The 30-Minute Money Plan for Moms

The

30-Minute

Money Plan for Moms

*How to Maximize Your Family
Budget in Minimal Time*

Catey Hill

CENTER
STREET

NEW YORK   NASHVILLE

Center Street
Hachette Book Group
1290 Avenue of the Americas, New York, NY 10104
centerstreet.com
twitter.com/centerstreet

First Edition: April 2018

Center Street is a division of Hachette Book Group, Inc. The Center Street name and logo are trademarks of Hachette Book Group, Inc.

The publisher is not responsible for websites (or their content) that are not owned by the publisher.

The Hachette Speakers Bureau provides a wide range of authors for speaking events. To find out more, go to www.HachetteSpeakersBureau.com or call (866) 376-6591.

Library of Congress Control Number: 2017959227

ISBNs: 978-1-4789-7565-6 (trade paperback), 978-1-4789-7566-3 (ebook), 978-1-5491-6833-8 (audiobook, downloadable)

Printed in the United States of America

LSC-C

10   9   8   7   6   5   4   3   2

E.B., I dedicate this book to you. You inspired it—and you continue to inspire me every day. And to my incredible, patient husband, without whom I never could have found the time and energy to write this book.

Contents

Introduction

Fellow mamas, if you're anything like me, motherhood thus far has been a series of surprises—most of them incredible and life-changing, but some of them (ahem, the cost!) not so much. Like your bod, which hasn't exactly bounced back, despite gulping down a revolting series of overpriced green juices for three straight days and completing (well, okay, "trying") a series of $20-a-pop spin classes. Seriously, if you wanted someone to yell at you, you'd just call your mom, who'd gladly do it for free. Or the fact that you haven't looked at your Visa bill in weeks, thanks to a late-night Zulily shopping spree. Admittedly, that wasn't the best idea while on unpaid maternity leave. And then there was that ill-advised go at organic cloth diapers (oh the places poop goes—especially when it isn't tightly contained by Pampers) that ended up breaking your washing machine. Your new perfume—a pungent mix of baby vomit, mashed carrots, and tops you didn't have time to take to the dry cleaners—means you're not exactly getting free coffee from that cute barista anytime soon. Oh, and the best part: Most of the time, you're too exhausted, and busy, to do anything about your ill-advised spending, let alone figure out the best way to save for college.

Or maybe your kids are a little older, and you're totally over those overpriced green juices. Your new "cleanse" involves sucking down the dredges of your kid's juice box so it doesn't leak all over the car. Zulily shopping sprees are a distant memory now that one trip to Target sets you back $200. Yes, all those baby expenses have just been replaced with new ones. You're dealing with summer camp, tutors, a constant stream of new clothes and toys, doctor's visits, and on, and on, and on . . . Sure, you knew kids were expensive, but the babysitting cost alone is enough to make you beg your doctor for a Xanax (just kidding—sort of!), especially now that yoga is out of the question. No amount of coffee can make a 6:30 a.m. yoga class on four hours of sleep anything other than risky for the people around you, and by 6:30 p.m., the only child's pose that'll make you happy involves your son posing in his bed fast asleep. And if someone brags about how she's already maxing out retirement savings or has Junior's college all paid for, the first image that runs through your head is her falling face-first into her homemade pie at the next bake sale.

Ladies, I get it. When I gave birth, I was bowled over and super stressed by how expensive it all was. And I write about money as my job! Who knew it would cost $500+ a year just to keep the child in diapers, and then hundreds more for the "educational" toys I feel like a bad mom if I don't buy. Then there's daycare and babysitting— how can watching a few babies sleep, cry, and poop command nearly as much as my first salary? And since when do teenage babysitters get well over minimum wage—even when I know they're just milking my Netflix subscription and Snapchatting their friends? There are doctor visits my insurance company somehow doesn't deem their problem to fully pay for. And, of course, there's wine, because seriously, who doesn't—between the projectile vomit, 3 a.m. feedings, and poop-smeared walls (yes, walls—this happens to almost every parent at least once!)—need a glass (or three) of Sauvignon Blanc?

It's not like you have time to deal with your not-so-amazing financial situation, right? You're lucky if you can pee by yourself and maybe get one hour with your spouse after the kids go to bed— during which time you inevitably fall asleep ten minutes into that

HBO show your childless friends have been telling you that you "must!!" watch.

You've seen the budgeting books that tell you to "track every purchase you make for the next couple months" and you think, *Come on! I can barely keep track of where my kids are within my own house, how in the heck am I going to do that?* Or how about those obviously childless "experts" who advise you to earn extra cash with a second job, or to put in a zillion extra hours for overtime or a big promotion. You're barely skating by on minimal sleep as it is! Plus, your kids are more important and you love spending time with them (well, except for that ten minutes a day that you spend crying in the bathroom from exhaustion and then the thirty minutes each night post-witching-hour that you spend wondering if they're secretly trying to ruin your life). You may need or want to work, but you don't want it to eat into family time too much. While that might not put you on the CEO track, you're okay with that. Or maybe you would like to walk outta that office door permanently, leaving the burned coffee, mind-numbing meetings, and reams of PowerPoint presentations squarely where they belong (the trash, thank you very much)—so you can devote yourself to your kids full time. But, you wonder, can you afford it? And what will that mean if you decide to go back to work down the road?

Kids are totally worth it (well, most of the time) but crazy expensive. So what's a busy mom—who doesn't have hours of time to track her spending or learn the ins and outs of college savings plans—to do? I dug into a ton of books to get some answers—and found that many of the books a mom seeking financial advice might pick up fall into just two categories.

The first type are the "super-couponer, mommy on budget" books about how to save money with advice that many of us either already know (use coupons, make one-dish meals), simply won't do (relinquishing your morning Starbucks is so not happening), or that don't save you enough money for all the effort it takes. Seriously, who has two hours a week to cut coupons only to save $4 at the grocery store?

The second type are often boring, overly complicated financial management books. Most of these are written for Americans in general, so they miss a lot of mom-specific issues. Plus, let's face it, you know you'll never actually slog through all those chapters. There's just something about the words "choosing investments for a 401(k) plan" that suddenly make you realize how much you need to color code your kids' sock drawers. Yes, their advice is great—build up an emergency fund, put away money for college for your kids, invest for your retirement, and on and on—but it's also often complicated, too time-consuming for most moms, and sometimes presented in a deadly boring way. It's also sure to leave you wondering: *Where is all this money coming from?* Because you know it's not from your current pray-there's-cash-in-there bank account?

I wanted a book that did both well. I wanted doable, meaningful ways to save significant money that I hadn't heard a million times already, or that didn't take up hours of time; and that showed me (in a non-deadly boring or overly complicated way) how to put those savings toward the things that would give my kids a better life. So I set out to write my own book. *The 30-Minute Money Plan* is designed to give busy moms the tools they need to budget smartly and save money so they can give their kids the best, be it an Ivy League education or a big yard to play in—while also making sure mama is taken care of herself (hello regular babysitters and getting to retire before you're ancient!).

I'll answer the questions no one else does, such as:

* What it *really* costs to raise a child each year, so you can budget accordingly. Because those online calculators, while fun to

play with, spit out numbers that won't even be close to right for many of us; nor is the government estimate of $245,000 to raise a child through age eighteen always accurate.

* How to deal with "mom guilt" (that thing that happens when your kid begs for a new Razor scooter and you start feeling like that might not be a bad idea thanks to that recent business trip you were forced to take) and "stroller envy" (when other moms are giving their kids the stuff you wish you could buy yours) so they don't destroy your budget.

* Some of the best new (and less pricey) ways to get professional help with all those not-always-riveting investment and savings issues so you don't have to think too much about making it all happen.

* And much more...

Okay, I know you are probably still feeling like this is way too big of a task to undertake. After all, it's not like you have hours of free time between getting the kids ready for school, shuttling them around to playdates and activities, doctors' visits, alone time with each kid, making dinner, cleaning up (even if that doesn't always happen), and of course, the dreaded mom butt–targeted workouts so you can finally squeeze into your prebaby jeans without having to slap on the Spanx, lie down, *and* pray!

Believe me, I hear you. But I also know this (because I've now done it): Managing your money smartly is totally doable even on a mom schedule. In fact, this book is specifically written for busy moms. Each chapter is broken into manageable chunks with easy-to-follow advice you can tackle in short periods of time. And whenever you can outsource something easily, I'll show you how. I swear, it won't bore you to death or totally freak you out. You'll get great, fast advice on how to save big on all those child-raising costs. And all the calculators and resources you need, as well as all the charts I highlight in this book and relevant updates, are easily down-loadable on my website at CateyHill.com, so you won't have to go hunting for them. I'll also help you develop a doable plan—that you can take care of in just thirty minutes a week—to set your family on the path to financial security.

Part I

How to Save Money without Losing Your Mind

Chapter 1

What It Costs to Raise Your Kids Each Year

You knew what to expect during practically every second of your pregnancy thanks to the deluge of books and (mostly unsolicited) "advice" that your mom and all her friends lorded upon you. Seriously, how many home remedies does one person need for stretch marks—especially considering none of them really work? You've practically memorized every childhood developmental milestone due to those stacks of "informational" pamphlets your overzealous pediatrician dumps on you. Frankly, they do more to send your anxiety levels through the roof—if she hasn't taken her first step at fourteen months and one day, will she be okay?!—than actually help you parent. Plus, thanks to all that practice you've been getting, you're now a total pro at looking like the picture of Zen, even as your child throws an Oscar-worthy, waterworks-filled tantrum in the grocery store. You know what I'm talking about: flinging herself on the dirty floor, fists flying, legs kicking, screaming she hates you because you won't buy her Fruity Pebbles. We've all been there!

But here's something you probably don't know, but should: what it will really cost you to raise that child (flying fists and all) through high school. Do you know what you will spend on food, clothing, childcare, education, and other essentials when he's a newborn versus an elementary school kid or older? What about the costs of all those extras you want for him, be it extracurriculars like music classes or his own bedroom in a home in a great school district? You may think you'll just wing it. After all, if you can get through college that way, can't you do the same with parenting? But I've seen many a mom accrue a pile of debt—and a bunch of gray hair!—while others have to work 24/7, just to pay for all the stuff they need. Because here's the thing: If you don't have a clue what these things will cost you (and they change a lot as your child gets older), there's almost no chance you can make a solid budget and start saving enough so you can afford to give your little munchkin the best life you can. Before you go there, the credit card is not a good answer. Getting an insane Visa bill in the mail when you're just barely skating by on eight hours of sleep—that's total, in the past two days!—is more than enough to send you sobbing into your pillow, again. Without a budget and a pile of savings, you risk going into debt and having to work well into your eighties (gulp!) or forgoing things you want (hello, finally seeing Bora Bora!) to pay it all off. If you think I'm exaggerating that you'll need to budget and save for your child's expenses, consider this: The average mom spends over $12,000 more per year—and this can ratchet up as the kids get older—once she has a child.

Before you start feeling like the worst mother in the world for not knowing and budgeting for these costs, you need to know: It's not your fault. There isn't a single source—not a media article, not an online calculator, not a book—that gives you accurate estimates of what it will cost to raise a child in each year of his life. Seriously, the best estimates out there come from the government, but thanks, in part, to the fact that their costs for childcare and education are way off for some of us, those numbers aren't even that helpful.

No one is giving moms an accurate answer to one of the biggest financial questions of their lives: How much will it cost me, each year, to raise a child? So I did a ton of research, calculations, and interviews to finally answer that question. I'm going to show you the kinds of costs that arise when you have a child and what the average mom spends on each. This will help you figure out what you should budget for each and whether your current spending is too high.

The Budget Breakdown: The Extra Money You'll Shell Out When You Have a Child

My friend came to me the other day with a dilemma. She and her husband had profited six figures when they sold the apartment her husband owned before they were married. They had hoped to keep this money in savings for a down payment on a house, but each month, they found themselves spending it—and she wasn't entirely sure why. "I'm not buying anything crazy," she said to me, which, as it turns out, was true. Their one-year-old son wasn't wearing designer clothes, except for a few fab (but free) hand-me-downs from her stylish friend in L.A.; he wasn't in some fancy-pants daycare. She was staying home with him for a year, which they'd budgeted for, and she barely used babysitters.

After a lengthy conversation about her spending, I learned that now that they had a child, they simply had significantly higher costs of living. They'd upgraded from their one-bedroom apartment rental to a two-bedroom (an extra $1,000+ a month), and between that, and the diapers (more than $500 over the course of her son's first year), food (more than $1,000 for the year even though she was breastfeeding him, too), and other extras, they were spending roughly $17,000 more than they were before the birth of their son.

If that $17,000 figure seems crazy to you, you'd better sit down for this part (and take a large gulp of wine while you're at it!). Moms who have a baby in daycare might spend an additional $19,000 or more per year (roughly $1,600 per month) on all the costs associated with raising a child, which include food and clothes for the kids, family-related transportation, an extra bedroom, childcare, education, health care, and miscellaneous stuff moms buy like goodies at the drugstore for the kiddies. Meanwhile, stay-at-home moms might spend an average of about $10,000 extra per year ($800 per month). Yes, that crazy discrepancy in cost between moms relying on daycare and stay-at-home moms is because daycare is ridiculously expensive with an average price tag of roughly $9,500, and it can go way higher. No joke, daycare now costs more than in-state college tuition in twenty-four states in the U.S., which means you'll pay someone more to watch your child sleep, poop, and scream than you will to shape their minds for a career!

The good news: Post-daycare, you'll get some relief. Once your child goes to school, expect to spend about $12,000 extra per year ($1,000 per month) per child when she's in elementary school, more than $13,000 a year (nearly $1,100 per month) extra in middle school and nearly $14,000 (nearly $1,200 a month) in high school. Does that help explain why your savings account is looking, um, pathetic these days? These numbers assume you have/will have two kids and are married. Parents with only children tend to spend a little more (roughly 25 percent more) and parents with three or more kids tend to spend a little less (roughly 25 percent less) per child. Single parents tend to spend a little less than married parents, as well.

While those numbers may be interesting to moms, some of the items that are included in those all-in tallies may not apply to your situation. For example, you may have gotten enough clothes for free from friends to last your little one through his first year, in which case the figures above wouldn't be that helpful to you, since they include the cost of clothing. That's why in this section I'm breaking out each of the eight costs associated with raising a child and tallying what you'll likely spend on each (based on what the average mom spends). We'll also look at how this changes as your child gets older. This can help you figure out what you might spend so you can start to budget accordingly. It's also a good guideline to see if there's an area where you've been spending too much. We'll also look at how costs differ between cities, since where you live is also a big factor.

Additional Cost #1: Food for the Kids

Assuming you don't habitually lose control in Whole Foods (seriously, how did that $9 hemp-and-flaxseed trail mix end up in your cart?) or treat GrubHub like your personal chef, you can expect to spend about $1,600 to $1,700 per year for food per kid for kids under about age four. These figures are what the average mom living in the U.S. spends, so they're a good gauge of whether your spending is too high and can help you make a clear budget going forward. For kids in elementary school, expect to spend about $2,300 to $2,700, for middle schoolers and high schoolers $2,800 per year, or more. This means that while you have young kids, you might only be shelling out $30 or so a week on food, but as they get older, these weekly expenditures can easily top $50.

Additional Cost #2: An Extra Bedroom

For many moms the additional cost of an extra bedroom is a non-negotiable expense. You love your child, but need plenty of separation from him post-7:30 p.m.! But it's going to cost you. The bulk—roughly 30 percent—of what it costs to raise a child is usually in the housing. What's more, according to ATTOM Data Solutions, the average cost for a home in a good school district is more than

70 percent higher (at around $343,000 across the nation; and way higher in pricey cities) than the average home for the U.S. overall, and that doesn't include potentially sky-high property taxes. For moms, this means that, in some cases, it can be more affordable to send your child to a private school than a public school (we'll talk more about this in Chapter 7).

The costs for an additional bedroom—either to rent or to buy a place with one—vary widely depending on where you live, and can range from just a few hundred extra bucks per month to $2,000 extra or more per month (I'm looking at you New York City and San Fran!).

What will it cost you personally? Because housing differs so much from city to city, you'll need to do your own calculations for your budget. If you plan to move to a good school district, first, look on sites like SchoolDigger.com and GreatSchools.com to find school districts that get good ratings. Then search on Trulia.com or Zillow .com for properties with the space you need in those districts to get an idea of prices. Compare the monthly cost you currently pay for your home to prices for the other homes you're thinking about buying. Bankrate.com has a great mortgage calculator that can tell you what you'll pay each month for homes at different price points. Don't forget to consider things like property taxes, which can be extremely high in a good school district.

Additional Cost #3: Clothes and Shoes for the Kids

On average, moms in America spend between $600 to $900 per year per child on clothes and shoes. Included in these figures for those with younger kids are diapers, which make up the bulk of your clothing costs in the early years at roughly $550 annually. If you're hooked on Zulily or Little Rue, you might spend way more, and less if you've got a huge network of friends donating clothes and shoes to you (which is super nice, but does tend to make you seriously question some people's taste...). The figures rise as your kids get older because clothing gets more expensive in larger sizes and your kids want and need more of it, including uniforms for sports and extracurriculars—and heaven help you if you have a teenage girl!

Additional Cost #4: Childcare

The last time I babysat for someone else's child (which admittedly, was about twenty years ago), I made about $4 an hour and the only real perk of my job was that I could raid the family's pantry and watch hours of TV once the kids went to sleep. Oh how times have changed! The going rate for a babysitter these days is now about $10 an hour and in many places a lot more. Experts say it's because parents expect more of their sitters these days. Gone are the days of the pantry raid, here to stay are babysitters with CPR training.

Daycare has its own heart-stopping cost: In some states, the average cost is around $8,000 per year for full-time daycare for an infant, in others it's more than $18,000. Because daycare and babysitting costs vary a lot depending on where you live, Chapter 5 has detailed estimates on what you might spend.

Additional Cost #5: Transportation for the Kids

I know you may hope that a sleek new Mercedes SUV is your future mom mobile, but I'm telling you: Just say no! I'm saying this not only because it's pricey, but also because, well...kids! Seriously, I don't know how they do it, but they can—and will—manage to get food wedged into every crevice, draw on the seats, spill chocolate ice cream and other unidentifiable substances on the carpet, and otherwise destroy a perfectly lovely automobile one messy day at a time. Plus, you'll be schlepping them everywhere—dance, tennis, soccer, art, you name it!—and that SUV will be guzzling gas (and thus your hard-earned cash) as you go. Because transportation costs for the average mom make up about 15 percent of the cost of raising a child—an additional $1,800 to $2,300 extra per year—you're going to want to save money in every way you can.[1]

Additional Cost #6: Education

When I was a kid, my mom just hustled me off to school with some pencils and a hot-pink-and-black Trapper Keeper (have I dated myself yet?) and called it a day. But teachers today send home huge lists of supplies that moms feel obligated to buy. Add in the costs of technology, and we're spending way more than our parents ever did. All told, this means that parents with kids in public school should budget a minimum of roughly $500 per year for younger children for education-related expenses, $700 for middle schoolers, and $900 or more for high school students; these figures could go much higher depending on your child's needs. These figures don't include extracurriculars, which we talk about below, or the new clothes your kids will be begging for as soon as they see what the cool kids are wearing on the first day of school (so much for all those clothes you bought them in July!). If you're thinking about private school, check out Chapter 7.

Additional Cost #7: Health Care for the Kids

Expect to spend a minimum of around $1,100 to $1,300 per year on health care costs for your child that aren't covered by insurance— things like prescription drugs and premiums that your employer

---

[1] For a two-parent, two-child household about 15 percent of your total transportation costs—including everything from gas to insurance to car wear-and-tear to car payments—are related to the kids, according to Census Bureau data.

doesn't pay. When you have a teenager, these costs go up: You can blame braces or other orthodontia for that. Data from American Express found that parents of middle-school kids spend an average of roughly $1,000 a year on braces. Of course, this can vary widely, depending on your child, of course, but also on your insurance plan, so call your HR department or insurance company to discuss your plan options, deductibles, and premium costs.

Additional Cost #8: Miscellaneous Items for the Kids

Moms should budget around $850 to $1,100 or more per year for random stuff—everything from toothbrushes to sports equipment—and in general, you can expect to spend less on this kind of stuff when the kids are little and more as they get older. One big factor that can drive up the costs in this category is what extracurriculars your kids participate in. On average, parents will spend roughly $450 per year on extracurriculars—and far more (as in, you can add an extra zero to that number) if your child participates in pricey sports. You'll find more details on this in Chapter 7. Another thing that can make this way more expensive is if you take the kids on a fun trip; I'll discuss travel savings in Chapter 9.

Meet the Mom Who Spends Less Than $20 a Week Raising Her Child

I've been following finance blogger Liz Frugalwoods for a couple years now, and I must admit that when I heard she'd had a baby in late 2015, I thought to myself: *Her frugality is going to change.* She's going to see that baby's face and start buying adorable clothes, educational books, organic everything. And no longer are she and her hubs going to retire in their thirties, as they'd planned.

Well, I couldn't have been more wrong. Frugalwoods has found a way to spend only about $75 per month on her daughter Estelle, so of course, I got her on the phone all the way from Vermont so she could share her secrets with you!

The first secret is that she gets almost everything—clothes, books, toys, crib, car seat, high chair, you name it—for free. "It's all hand-me-downs," she says. I know you're thinking to yourself, well, of course, hand-me-downs are the way to go to save money. But Frugalwoods takes it to a new level. She says that most people, once they are done having kids, want all the stuff out of their house. She takes the whole lot of it. "We take anything that is offered—and if we don't need it, we pass it along," she says. So she'd take a pile of stuff from family or a friend's house, sift through it, and either take it for her daughter or donate it. Yes, this takes some time, but because it can save you hundreds of dollars, this approach can be worth it. She also gets stuff from the "Buy Nothing Project" (BuyNothingProject.org), where people give and receive items to one another for free, which has chapters across the country. And she checks out books from her local library rather than buying them.

She says she's doesn't worry much if the clothes have stains or are boys' clothes, pointing out that her daughter will likely get them dirty herself pretty quickly anyway. She also doesn't fret over not having the latest toys for Estelle: She makes Estelle toys out of things like yogurt containers, and gets plenty of used items that she just cleans before giving them to her daughter. "At the end of the day, all that she wants is to be with us and to have that interaction," Frugalwoods says. And when Estelle is older and asks for specific things, Frugalwoods says that she and her husband will "try to find the item for free or used (from a garage sale or thrift store), we'll discuss whether it's a need or a want, we'll see if we can borrow it from a friend (if it's a short-term use item), or [Estelle] can ask for it for her birthday or Christmas."

Of course, being a worried mom myself, I pointed out to her that experts say not to buy a used crib and car seat because it can be dangerous if they've been damaged or in an accident. She got around this, too: She got hers from a trusted, dear friend who assured her the items hadn't been in an accident or damaged in any way. She also checked online for both to make sure there had been no recalls associated with them.

Frugalwoods also only does free activities with Estelle, and she says that they're easy to find even though she lives in rural Vermont. She looks at local libraries and hospitals for events like storytimes and music hour and on local parents' Facebook groups. She also organizes playgroups herself.

So what does Frugalwoods buy? "Just consumables," she says— things like milk, food, medicine, diapers, and wipes. She periodically price checks these things, but doesn't do it each time she shops; she says that's simply too annoying (Go Liz! I totally agree). Here's what she spends money on: Organic milk from warehouse club BJ's ($9 per month); food from various places including BJ's and Hannaford's ($30 to $50 per month); store-brand diapers from Walmart ($17.50 per month; 12 cents per diaper); bulk wipes from BJs ($6); baby Motrin ($2 per month; replaces roughly every three months), diaper rash cream ($4); and Vaseline ($2). To save on food, she makes her own baby food and Estelle generally just eats what they eat beyond that.

Admittedly, because Liz and her hubby both work from home it does help shave costs, since they don't need to pay for childcare, and her husband's firm pays for the entirety of their health care. Still, I'm impressed by Frugalwoods's dedication to never buying anything new but consumables. She didn't even buy Estelle anything for her birthday or Christmas, and says that once her daughter is old enough to want things for the holidays, she will probably still buy them used at garage sales.

For Frugalwoods, this is doing more than helping her and her husband save money, it's teaching Estelle an important life lesson. As Frugalwoods told me in an interview I did with her for Market-Watch: "I think it is teaching her to value things other than money, other than consumption...I want her to be focused on what she can do in this world, not what she can buy." What's more, the frugality is good for the whole family. "Our goal with our frugality isn't to save every dollar possible," she says, "it's to optimize and create efficiencies and only spend on the things that bring us lasting joy." Amen to that.

A City-by-City Look at the Costs of Raising a Child

Freelance writer Linda Formichelli can easily list all the things she loves about Concord, New Hampshire: The incredible network of moms she met through a parents' meetup group; the 1900s home she and her husband bought and renovated; Concord's quintessentially New England downtown with its quirky longtime residents. So when Linda told me she'd decided to move, my first thought was *How could you?*

A big part of that decision came down to money: "I wanted to cut down on my hours at work so I could spend more time with my son," she explained to me. But the high cost of living in Concord prevented her from doing that. Each month, Linda shelled out nearly $2,000 for her mortgage, $500 for heating in the winter, and $600 for two-day-a-week childcare. The massive amounts of snow didn't help matters, either—one winter it topped ten feet! So after a visit with her parents, who had recently moved to Cary, North Carolina, Linda packed up her family and headed south—a move that she says saves her about $18,000 per year. Her parents now help with childcare, her mortgage is roughly $500 cheaper per month, and everything from taxes to health insurance to utilities costs less. While there are plenty of things Linda misses about Concord—the friends she'd made up there chief among them—she says she doesn't regret her move, as she now works less and spends more time with her son. "Things were just so expensive in Concord," she says. "It would have been harder to make that work."

After hearing Linda's story, I spent a few weeks dreaming of how my life might be different in a cheaper-than-New-York city like New Orleans (*Wouldn't my daughter look so cute toddling around a little court-yard?*) or Atlanta (*Hi Mom, want to babysit every Friday and Saturday night?*). I know other moms would do it, too. After all, who hasn't dreamed of packing up and moving to some inexpensive little town near the beach where you could far more easily manage your family's life? Of course, I, like most of you, will probably never leave the city we live in. We all have jobs and friends and other ties to where we live.

Still, we all need to know what it will cost us to raise our children where we live, so we can budget accordingly. So here is what the average mom in different cities spends to raise her kids. Note that most of the variation is due to the differing costs of housing and childcare, and these costs include full-time daycare. These numbers also include all the costs we talked about above (but do not include college savings or private school costs—see Chapter 7 for those). If your city isn't on this list, don't worry, I've got you covered. My website has info for other cities, as well as urban regions (e.g., what people who live in say an average Midwestern city spend), and rural areas. My site also has costs without daycare. These numbers are rounded off and are just rough estimates, of course, but are a great place to start figuring out how to budget.

How Much It Will Cost to Raise a Child Through Age 17 by City

METRO AREA	TOTAL COST
Atlanta, GA	$296,000
Austin, TX	$293,000
Baltimore, MD	$342,000
Boston, MA	$436,000
Charleston, SC	$296,000
Charlotte, NC	$292,000
Chicago, IL	$359,000
Cincinnati, OH	$273,000
Cleveland, OH	$297,000
Columbus, OH	$274,000
Dallas, TX	$298,000
Denver, CO	$338,000
Des Moines, IA	$273,000
Detroit, MI	$284,000
Hartford, CT	$364,000
Honolulu, HI	$522,000
Houston, TX	$286,000

METRO AREA	TOTAL COST
Indianapolis, IN	$274,000
Jacksonville, FL	$279,000
Kansas City, KS/MO	$280,000
Las Vegas, NV	$315,000
Little Rock, AR	$264,000
Los Angeles, CA	$420,000
Louisville, KY	$266,000
Miami, FL	$326,000
Milwaukee, WI	$308,000
Minneapolis, MN	$322,000
Nashville, TN	$281,000
New Orleans, LA	$284,000
New York (Manhattan), NY	$634,000
Oklahoma City, OK	$251,000
Omaha, NE	$274,000
Philadelphia, PA	$345,000
Phoenix, AZ	$289,000
Pittsburgh, PA	$281,000
Portland, OR	$388,000
Providence, RI	$353,000
Raleigh, NC	$285,000
Richmond, VA	$279,000

(Continued)

METRO AREA	TOTAL COST
San Diego, CA	$421,000
San Francisco, CA	$530,000
Seattle, WA	$429,000
St. Louis, MO	$267,000
Tampa, FL	$267,000
Tulsa, OK	$263,000
Washington, D.C.	$431,000

Sources: Council for Community and Economic Research; Census Bureau; Child Care Aware; Care.com. Assumes a middle-income house and up and that this is/will be a two-parent, two-child household in an urban area. All figures are approximate.

If, after reading this, you've begun to drown your sorrows in wine (been there!), I totally get it. But I'm here to help: We're going to look at ways to save in each category I mentioned in this chapter. After reading the next nine chapters, you'll be able to shave $1,000 or more off the total cost of raising your children each year.

Chapter 2

Food

Super Supermarket Saving

I'm going to make a few assumptions. You're not one of those moms who has hours to spend clipping coupons simply to save fifty cents on a jar of pasta sauce or a pound of turkey. And you aren't one of those patient saints who compares every single can of beans available on the grocery shelf to find which one might save you ten cents. Nor will you vow to never go out to dinner ever again just to save a bit of money (um, mommy having to cook seven days a week = mommy meltdown...). Am I on track?

The good news is you don't have to become an obsessive coupon-clipping, price-comparing shopper to save a pile of money on food this year. You don't have to give up occasional indulgences, either. Because this chapter is going to dish on little-known ways to cut your food and grocery expenses, saving you at least a couple hundred dollars every year—without too much effort. Most of these tips are either fast and easy to do, or, if they take longer, they're financially worth it for the time they take. Nearly every tip in here allows you to save you upward of $50 per year. The ones that might not save you that much are literally so easy (I'm talking mere seconds of your time), that I included them simply because they're no-brainers.

Why Coupons Are Often a Trap

Coupons can save you money—and I know many people who use them well. But there's a reason that brands and stores issue so many of them (and it is NOT out of the goodness of their hearts!). Coupons are designed to lead you to spend more than you might have otherwise, and stay loyal to a store or brand even when it isn't saving you money.

One study, published in 2003, entitled "Spending More to Save More: The Impact of Coupons on Premium-Priced Product" showed that "consumers often spend more while attempting to save money" using coupons. In the study, more than one out of four people who used a coupon ended up increasing their spending rather than decreasing it. Consumers tend to focus on the savings that the coupon seems to give them (ohhh, $1 off!) rather than the total they will end up paying for the item versus other comparable items. A 2014 study from coupon site RetailMeNot found that "55 percent of smartphone coupon users will spend more money during their online or in-store visit—the majority at least $25 more. Additionally, 77 percent of customers will spend between $10 and $50 more than anticipated, and 17 percent will spend an extra $50 or more." What's more, the survey revealed that "receiving a deal or savings opportunity via a digital coupon can be the tipping point for a consumer to click 'buy' online or to walk into a store and make the purchase in person. Nearly 80 percent of respondents agreed that digital coupons 'close the deal' for them when undecided on a purchase." In other words: Coupons may lead you to buy something—and spend more on it—than you normally would.

What's more, a study of digital coupons by market research firm Forrester found that roughly eight in ten consumers are likely to become repeat buyers of a certain brand when that brand offers coupons or promotional offers. When you become a "repeat buyer" of a certain brand, you often go on autopilot when you're shopping, just grabbing that brand no matter the actual cost you will pay.

Look, I'm not saying never use coupons. I'll even give you some coupon tips later in this chapter because they can, and do, save moms money, sometimes a lot of it. But you have to be careful. Ask yourself *Do I need this item?* and *Would I be buying this kind of thing if it wasn't for a coupon?* Often the answer is no—you're just enticed by what seems to be a deal and buying because of it.

The New Rules of Grocery Shopping

The average family can easily spend $150 and up a week just on groceries—and you likely spend way more if, a) you're like most moms I know who buy plenty of healthy goodies and organic food, or b) gets Whole Foods–ed (that's what happens when you buy a tiny handful of things for more than $50). So cutting spending at the grocery store could be one of the most important ways to save money for your family—just behind cutting a huge expense like your housing cost, which isn't that easy to do quickly (and, let's face it, you're pretty obsessed with your CB2 furnished loft at the moment).

Many moms I know spend a lot of time hunting for coupons to save money at the grocery store. If you have the time to do that, great, but I find I don't. Seriously, if I spend one hour a week looking for grocery coupons, I might save $10 total; but my time is more valuable than that! I'm worth at least $15 an hour—well, except for after 8 p.m. when all I can manage to do is watch *Grey's Anatomy* and drink a glass of wine.

The point is, there are much better ways to save. This section gives you the ten new rules for shopping at the grocery store that won't eat into your valuable time, and a bunch of additional tips along the way. Learn and follow these rules from here on out, and you'll automatically save at the grocery store—without having to really think about it.

THE ONE THING

If You Only Do One Thing to Save on Food Costs, Do This

Avoid food shopping at the grocery store when possible. Most shoppers don't know the prices of most of the items they buy at the grocery store, but in general, tend to remember (at least roughly) the prices of four commonly bought things: milk, eggs, bananas, and loaves of bread. So grocery stores often trick you into thinking they have low prices by keeping prices for these items pretty low. But here's the thing: Despite those items often having decently low prices, in general, you pay more for food at the grocery store than at other spots.

I know that, in the back of your head, you probably understand this but it bears repeating: Instead of food shopping at the grocery store, opt to food shop as much as you can at Costco, Sam's, and other warehouse clubs, as well as Target and Walmart (which now carry tons of organic items). All of these places frequently

have better prices on food—without your having
to scour circulars or coupon sites—than your local
grocery store. This alone will save you at least $200
per year on your grocery bill without you having to
think about it much. Drive the extra way if you have
to. It may cost a few extra bucks in gas, but it's usually
worth it.

Should you find yourself in a drugstore like
Walgreens, Rite Aid, or Duane Reade (which is
generally a no-no, see page 152), you might as well
check for great deals on staples like milk and eggs, as
they often put these on special so that they're even
cheaper than at the grocery store—sometimes up to
40 percent cheaper. This is usually a marketing ploy
to get you to think of the store as more than just a
place to buy shampoo and Advil. This is not, I repeat
NOT, worth making a special trip for—those stores are
designed for you to grab more than you'd planned—
but if you're in there already, take a look. *Average
savings: More than $200 per year.*

1. Buy Frozen without Sacrificing Freshness (No, Really!)

Fish are often laid out over ice at the fish counter, which makes
them look fresh-caught. But often they were previously frozen to
keep them fresh while they were on the boat and then thawed at the
store. Buy that same fish in the frozen aisle, and you can save as much
as 40 percent. If the grocery store is behaving on the up-and-up, on
the "fresh" fish you will see (typically in teeny print on the sign label-
ing the fish) a note that says "fresh frozen" or something like that,

but not all stores label their fresh fish like that. To make frozen fish taste fresher, thaw it in a bowl of milk (this helps remove that frost-bitten taste).

Fruits and vegetables, like the apples, berries, onions, and other items lining the produce section of your grocery store seem bright and fresh, but they're often not. One study found that the average apple in the grocery store was fourteen months old (um, gross!). How can that be? Fruits are often picked and then immediately put into cold storage for months until stores need them; once they do, they are brought out and put on the produce shelf to masquerade as fresh-picked produce—which is then marked up accordingly. Even organic markets do this; it's not just the big chain grocery stores. To avoid this, buy what's local and in season at the time because those items are far less likely to have met the cold-storage fate. If you want an item that isn't in season or local, consider buying it frozen and saving a bunch by doing so, without sacrificing flavor. *Average savings: $150 per year.*

---

2 Savvy Shopping Tips That Take 2 Seconds to Do

While neither of these tips is likely to save you a ton of money, because they literally take two seconds to do, I think they're worth mentioning.

1. Press the padding around meat.

   Meat is one of the priciest things shoppers buy, so you might as well be getting the freshest meat while you're at it. To determine this, push down on the padding that's lining the bottom of the Styrofoam tray that's holding the red meat or chicken; if a lot of juice comes out, it's probably been sitting for a while and you should opt for another, fresher piece to avoid having to toss meat that doesn't taste so great.

2. Steer clear of the mister.

Grocery stores love to mist their produce, as it makes it glisten and seem ultra-fresh. While that dewy look may tempt you, beware: All that water is merely adding unnecessary weight to your produce, and most produce is sold by weight. It also sometimes means it's quicker to rot. Instead, opt for items that aren't directly under the mister.

2. Put the Butcher to Work

It may not be a surprise that it's almost always cheaper to buy a large hunk of meat—be it a flank steak or a chuck roast—than it is to buy the item precut. But here's what many people don't know and don't do: Buy that large hunk of meat and then ask the butcher to cut it, grind it, or debone it for you. The people working behind the meat counter are almost always willing to do this for you, you're getting the same meat as if you'd bought it precut, and it can save you 30 percent or more. *Average savings: $50 per year.*

3. Beware: The Same Item May Be Priced Vastly Differently Even within the Same Store at the Same Time

Don't expect to pay the same price for certain items, especially things like nuts and cheese—even if you buy them at the same time from the same store. For example, buying cheese in the dairy, deli, or cheese specialty section can result in you paying prices that vary by up to 50 percent, with the specialty cheese department likely the priciest of all followed by the deli department. The reason: Different departments in the store have different overhead costs. The deli and specialty cheese departments have more staff to pay typically, so they price identical items differently. *Average savings: $50 per year.*

4. Shop Left

Grocery stores are super sneaky in their design, as many are set up so that you enter toward the right and then go counterclockwise around the store buying items. The reason: Most of us are right-handed and we grab more with our right hand than left hand, so this design lures us into spending more. Buck that trend by shopping the opposite way (in other words, go left). *Average savings: $100 per year.*

Stock Up on This $1 Magic Ingredient

Baking soda: The stuff is a lifesaver. While you probably know to use it to do things like clean your fridge and sink and deodorize the diaper pail and your kids' smelly shoes, here's what you're not using it for (but should):

- Clean produce. If you're anti-pesticides (and seriously, who isn't?), wash the fruits and veggies you give the kids with cold water and a touch of baking soda; rinse well.
- Get crayon off the walls easily. Dip a washcloth in some baking soda and that should take it right off. To erase pen marks on the wall, try white vinegar, which can also help remove stickers and price tags that the kids have stuck there.
- Cleaner dishes. Add a couple tablespoons to your dishwashing detergent, and you'll get noticeably cleaner dishes. This is great if you're like me and can't stand how baby bottles don't seem to get clean in the dishwasher.
- Cleaner clothes. Add about a half cup to your usual wash (you can use a little less laundry detergent when

you do this) and you'll notice that your clothes get cleaner. You may also want to do this with new baby clothes to better remove chemicals. Just be sure your laundry detergent is baby-friendly.

- Cleaner a lot of things. The family's toothbrushes get super germy—clean by letting them soak in a solution of half baking soda and half water overnight; rinse well and then you're good to go! You can also use it to clean your hairbrush! Mix about a tablespoon of baking soda into a bowl of warm water and soak your brush that way.

5. Rethink Your Shopping Timing

The less often you grocery shop, the less you spend, studies show. The average household makes 1.6 trips a week, so cut down your trips to the store. You can make a once-a-week trip count even more by doing it on a Tuesday or Wednesday. While the most popular day to shop, not surprisingly, is Saturday, you'll likely get a better selection and can best take advantage of sales if you shop on a Tuesday or Wednesday. Don't worry, you can just show up—and of course already be a member of the store's loyalty program—and take advantage of the sales then; no hunting for coupons required! The reason: Many stores (though this does vary from store to store; ask a sales clerk if you aren't sure at your store) start their weekly discounts and promotions on one of these two days, so shopping then let's you take advantage of the items before they run out. To save even more, go after work and have Dad watch the kids at home. Studies show that shopping with other people ups your spending. Added bonus: You get an hour free of whining! *Average savings: $150 per year.*

6. Don't Buy Paper Goods or Household Items at the Grocery Store

While food isn't always the best deal at the grocery, paper products and other household items like cleaning products (unless they are on clearance or in a big-time sale) tend to be even worse deals at the grocery store. For bargain basement prices on things like paper plates and napkins, run into the dollar store. If that's not your style or the quality is crucial (if you're thinking sloppy joes at your barbecue, don't dollar store it!), warehouse clubs, Walmart, and Target are your next best bets for everything from paper towels to toilet paper to laundry detergent. *Average savings: $50 per year.*

7. Get Smart about Organic

Most of us moms want to buy organic when we can, but it's super pricey to fill your cart with it. So here's how to do that effectively.

Some organic milk is a great buy (unless your family blows through milk in mere days) because though it can be double the price of nonorganic milk, it usually lasts twice as long. The reason: It's often subjected to ultra-high temperature processing (it will note that it is UHT on the carton), which means that it's been heated to very high temperatures to kill more bacteria; that gives it a longer life. Nonorganic milk is much less likely to have undergone this process.

Here's another secret: The Environmental Working Group (EWG .org) does studies on which foods have the most and least pesticides on them, which can help you figure out what's worth buying organic and what's not. In 2017, they listed foods with the least pesticides (and thus those that you can more safely buy as nonorganic).

Produce with the Least Pesticides

asparagus

avocados

cabbage

cantaloupe

cauliflower

eggplant

grapefruit

honeydew melon

kiwis

mangoes

onions

papayas

pineapples

sweet corn

sweet peas

You also may want to avoid buying organic quinoa, because all quinoa is naturally coated with a substance that keeps pests at bay, which means quinoa is often grown using fewer pesticides anyway.

On the flipside, "more than 98 percent of samples of strawberries, spinach, peaches, nectarines, cherries, and apples tested positive for residue of at least one pesticide," according to EWG—which means organic versions of these may be the way to go.

Finally, if you see seafood labeled "organic," know this: While the USDA regulates the use of this term when it comes to produce and meat, it does not regulate it with regards to seafood. That means that just because your seafood says organic, it doesn't mean it was raised with the standards you might think. *Average savings: $75 per year.*

Quick Tip

Go vegetarian once a week. Your kids might not like it, but I promise you eating pasta or all veggies once a week won't kill them. *Average savings per year: $250.*

---

8. Pop in Your Headphones—and Speed Up Your Heart Rate

Ever noticed how your grocery store is constantly playing slow elevator music? That's on purpose. Studies show that slow music slows down shoppers, who then buy more. Plus, they place end-of-aisle displays throughout the store to keep you dawdling. Stop falling for those tricks! Pop in headphones with peppy music (Beyoncé does the trick for me!), pull out your list—organized by aisle so you don't have to double back through; you can use an app like Grocery iQ to help you do this—and start stopping quickly. Added bonus: You'll burn at least a few extra calories without having to suffer through the hell of CrossFit! *Average savings: $50 per year (better booty not included!).*

9. Use This Time-Saving Coupon Strategy

By now, you know how I personally feel about coupons. But that's me. I know some moms can—and do—use coupons responsibly. Sites like Coupons.com and apps Favado are super easy to use, or just peek in your grocery store's circular to see if you can save. Many stores, like Target and Kroger, allow you to clip virtual coupons in their store apps either by searching by name or scanning items. Then you just scan your personal bar code at the register to automatically use all applicable coupons.

While it's often far too annoying and time-consuming to try to find coupons for everything on your shopping list, there are some items that almost always have a coupon available for them. If these goodies are on your shopping list, it may pay to do a quick scan for coupons. According to Coupons.com in 2017, here are the four food categories that most commonly have coupons and their average values:

a. Breakfast foods ($0.89)
b. Snack foods ($0.96)
c. Frozen foods ($1.13)
d. Cheese ($0.86)

Fresh fruits and veggies don't tend to have a lot of coupons but that doesn't mean you shouldn't buy them! Keep an eye out for sales on frozen produce—especially those easy microwave-in-the-bag ones—and stock up!

Finally, this may be a bridge too far for some of you (totally get it!) but you can get paid to shop without much effort with apps like Ibotta and Checkout 51. Buy certain items at the store, snap a pic of your receipt with your smartphone and send that pic to them, and they will send money right to a PayPal account. No coupon-laden spiral notebook needed! Now, if only you could get paid to visit Saks. *Average savings per year: $50.*

Become a Less Wasteful Family

One of the most annoying things for any mom (besides trying to get your child to eat anything green) is buying a bunch of food and then having to toss it because it spoiled.

The first thing to know is that while expiration dates matter for fresh items like meats and milk, for many processed foods, they're not that relevant. That means you can stop feeling guilty about that time you gave your kids year-old potato chips! The expiration dates on canned foods, cereals, and many snacks are merely a suggestion from the manufacturer for the best flavor. So while things like chips, cereals, and canned beans may lose some of their flavor months after the "best if used by" label says so (and often this doesn't even happen), they usually aren't harmful to eat if you've kept them in a place like your pantry, which is dry and out of direct sunlight. This means that moms don't have to toss these kinds of snacks right after they expire.

The average American wastes twenty pounds of food every month—and in doing so is literally throwing away hundreds of dollars a year. Here's how to start fixing that.

Make these foods last longer:

* Cheese: Smear butter on the sides of the cheese so it doesn't dry out. Wrap in parchment paper with foil over that and leave it in the crisper drawer.
* Tomato paste: Most recipes only call for a bit of tomato paste, so you waste the whole can but you don't have to. Put one tablespoon dollops of tomato paste on a piece of wax paper and freeze them like that; then pop all the dollops into a plastic bag and store in the freezer.
* Fresh bread: Leave it in the paper bag it comes in and it will get stale quickly (just what the grocery store is hoping for); instead, pop into an airtight plastic bag.
* Onion: If you only use part of an onion, keep the unused part fresh by rubbing it with butter before wrapping in aluminum foil and popping into the fridge.

* Fruits and veggies: Place dry sponges along the bottom of your veggie bins in the fridge to absorb the excess moisture that makes fruits and veggies rot faster.
* Cake: Keep cake from drying out by storing it with half an apple.
* Brown sugar: If your brown sugar has gotten hard, put it in a sealed ziplock bag with a piece of bread and in about a day, it will be soft again.
* Lettuce: If your lettuce has gotten a bit soggy, fill a bowl with cold water and squeeze a couple tablespoons of lemon juice in it. Submerge the lettuce, then pop into the fridge for about an hour.

Never Throw Out These 5 Things

1. **Honey:** They found it in still-edible form in Egyptian tombs, due to its low moisture, high acidity, and hydrogen peroxide content.
2. **White sugar:** If you store it in a sealed, moisture-free bag, it will stay fresh thanks to its resistance to microbial growth.
3. **Liquor:** Though it's not like that vodka isn't going into your martinis this very year!
4. **Vinegar:** Just keep it in a cool spot like a dark pantry.
5. **Pure salt:** The addition of ingredients like iodine to salt may make it expire sooner.

Finally, you often don't need to use the full recommended amount of laundry detergent and dishwashing liquid; try using about two-thirds of what you usually do, most likely you won't notice the difference.

Momsanity Tip: Get Your Groceries Delivered

I know you're probably thinking this is only for people who live in New York and San Francisco, or people with a ton of money, but the reality is that there are now relatively affordable grocery delivery services for cities all over the country. Unfortunately, they're harder to find in smaller towns, though more local grocery stores are offering it, and regional services are popping up in many places. My mom lives in the suburbs of Atlanta and I just found one for her. When we compared the prices to those at her local grocery store, they were about equal.

Here's another thing to add to the "pros" column: The people who use an online grocery service like it. Data out in 2017 from research firm NPD Group found that more than 60 percent are "completely satisfied" by the experience, just 6 percent were either "neutral" or "dissatisfied." The rest were somewhat satisfied. The reason most people were pleased by it shouldn't surprise you: convenience. Though they also mentioned good delivery options, shipping deals, and good assortment of items.

Should you consider it? Ask yourself: Does grocery shopping take a big chunk of time out of your week that you'd rather spend with your family or friends? If so, it's worth considering.

But you have to weigh the cost versus the benefit by considering these potential issues:

* **Delivery or membership fee:** Almost all of these services charge a delivery fee (usually ranging from about $5 to $14 per delivery) and/or an annual membership fee (usually $150 to $299 per year, which breaks out to anywhere from $12.50 to about $25 a month). They may also require minimum orders, typically about $50 (though with a family, I've

found that I usually easily meet the minimums without even blinking).

* **Food upcharge:** There may be an upcharge on the products they offer for delivery. Make sure this doesn't happen by keeping one receipt from your last grocery shopping trip to an actual store and popping on their site to make sure the prices are comparable. For me, the $6 delivery fee my service charges is worth it; it never blows my budget and it saves me about an hour and a half of time a week. The prices for my service are often less than my local grocery store (win!), but this is by no means the case for most people.

* **Picking your own fruits, veggies, and meat:** This is the part that most annoys me: You can't pick your own fruits, meat, and veggies. My local service does a decent job of selecting ripe items (and things get eaten quickly in my house anyway), but it's important to know what the delivery service's policy is should they deliver you bruised fruits, wilted veggies, or an unacceptable piece of meat. Will they refund you without many questions asked? If they don't do a good job of selecting fresh items and it's going to be a hassle to address it, a service like this may prove a waste of money for you.

* **Options:** These options won't be available for everyone but it's worth checking in your area for the following providers if grocery delivery intrigues you:
  o Amazon Fresh
  o Harris Teeter
  o Instacart
  o Kroger
  o Peapod
  o Safeway
  o Vons
  o Walmart

Because the terms of each of these providers change, I'm not going to list them here. But I will say this: You must look both at the membership fee and the cost of the items closely. When I reviewed these, some had a high membership fee but lower prices on goods, and others had lower membership fee but higher prices on goods.

Chapter 3

Housing

Home Sweet (Affordable) Home

If you're like most moms I know, housing costs—everything from your mortgage or rent to utilities and cable—suck up about one-quarter or more of the family paycheck each month. Whew! It's enough to make you dream of a big, fat trust fund every time you pay that mortgage. Obviously, the most significant way to cut housing-related expenses is to move somewhere cheaper (I'm going to talk about an inspiring family who downsized and changed their lives on page 50). But let's get real here: Moving to a smaller, less desirable home in a worse school district probably isn't something you're willing to do. Frankly, you can't stop dreaming about a home with a big yard for the kids to play in, maybe with a weeping willow and a tire swing. Don't worry, you don't have to move or give up your big yard dreams, as I'll show you other ways to save on everything from utilities to insurance to repairs.

THE ONE THING

If You Only Do One Thing to Save on Housing Costs, Do This

Here's a secret to save you tens of thousands (yep, you read that right!) on your housing costs: Avoid the "recommendation trap." A study published in the *Journal of Real Estate Finance and Economics* found that women, on average, pay more for mortgages than men, with average mortgage interest rates 0.4 percent higher than for men. For a thirty-year mortgage on an average home, the difference between a 5 percent rate and a 5.4 percent rate is $26,000 (that could pay college tuition for a year at some schools!). The authors say this is likely because women, more than men, choose lenders by recommendation, while men tend to search for the lowest rate (and there's probably some bias against us ladies going on there, too). The solution: Get at least five quotes for your mortgage interest rate when buying or refinancing your home. Look into refinancing your home if you could drop your mortgage interest rate by at least a half of a percentage point; Bankrate.com has a great calculator that can help you figure this out and whether its financially worth it to do this when you factor in all the refinancing fees. Use a simple site like LendingTree .com or Bankrate.com to get a bunch of quotes in one easy spot. Don't feel like searching for a mortgage yourself? I'll talk about the pros and cons of using a mortgage broker on page 190. *Average savings: More than $850 per year.*

Utilize Utility Savings

When it comes to utilities, you spend most of your money on keeping the house and the shower at the right temperature.

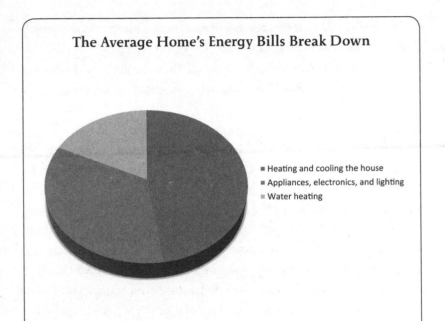

The Average Home's Energy Bills Break Down

- Heating and cooling the house
- Appliances, electronics, and lighting
- Water heating

Heating and cooling the house: 47.7 percent
Appliances, electronics, lighting: 34.6 percent
Water heating: 17.7 percent
Source: Department of Energy.

That's why these basics are so important:

✴ Check your home for air leaks. Add appropriate weather-stripping on windows and doors and plug up any holes.

 * Change heating and air filters regularly. This is annoying but necessary. Google the type of filter you have to figure out how often it needs to be changed, or get reusable ones.
 * Install programmable thermostats.
 * Keep the water heater at 120°F.

Check out the Energy.gov site. Right on their homepage you will find a ton more tips on how to save money on energy.

Okay, maybe you already knew all that. So let's look at what many homeowners miss. Here are six ways you can save on monthly utility bills.

1. Get a Free Energy Audit

Some cities offer residents a free energy audit, during which an expert will come out to your house and let you know if you could save money on your water and/or electricity bill. The auditor will examine your home—including appliances, insulation, heating system, cooling system, filters, windows, and more—to see what you can do to slash your energy usage (and the costs surrounding them). A quick Google search of your city's name and "free energy audit" will tell you if you can get one for free. Even if it's not free, it's often worth having one done—especially if you feel your bills are too high—as this can save you hundreds of dollars each year. The audit itself will take anywhere from forty-five minutes to three hours, and if you implement the recommendations, you can save as much as $600 a year (depending on how energy efficient your house already is), according to the U.S. Department of Energy. *Average savings: up to roughly $600 per year.*

2. Beware of Energy Vampires

You probably already know that energy efficient appliances and lightbulbs can save you money in the long term, but you may not know this: About 10 percent of the average household's energy bill comes from so-called vampire appliances—appliances that you leave plugged in while not in use. That might cost you $250 or more per year. Flat-screen TVs are the worst energy vampire of them all, sometimes costing you up to about $160 just when you aren't using them. Of course, it's unlikely you will unplug your flat screen when it's not in use, but there's another way to stop this energy suckage: Use what's called an advanced power strip (you can order them on Amazon or another online site for about $15), which keeps appliances from sucking out so much energy when they're on but not in use. Also plug your kids' video game consoles (these waste up to about $75 per year), DVRs, and cable boxes (each up to about $22 per year), and computers (up to about $40 each per year) into these strips.

Leaving easy-to-unplug kitchen appliances like coffeemakers and Cuisinarts, as well as cell phone chargers plugged in also wastes money. Though it's usually only about $5 per year per appliance, those all add up. Since they're so easy to unplug after use, you might as well do it. If you're curious how much energy—and money—each of your specific devices eats up, the Belkin Conserve Insight Energy Use Monitor will give you more precise estimates of what each item is costing you after you pop in your electricity company's rates. You plug it in to the same outlet as the device is plugged into and it reads electricity usage. You can buy this device on Amazon for about $30, and there are other, similar devices from other companies, too. *Average savings: $250 per year.*

Why You Should Run Your Appliances at Night

While this tip may not save most people a ton, it's super simple to do, so I want to throw it out there. Some utility companies charge more during the day—when most people run their appliances—than at night. Make a quick call to your utility company and ask if they have different rates and when they apply. If they say yes, do your laundry, run your dishwasher, et cetera when rates are low to save money. I love this tip because while it probably isn't going to save you hundreds (though I have seen cases where night rates are two-thirds less than day rates), it literally takes you no extra time; just simply switch your chores timing.

3. Install an Irrigation Meter

The average household in America spends about $40 per month on water/sewer—far more in some cities. What's more, you get charged twice for water/sewer: One time when it comes into your home, and another when it gets pumped out into the sewer. But because not all water will hit the sewer—like the water you use to water your lawn or fill the pool or hot tub—there's no reason you need to always get charged twice. That's where an irrigation meter comes in. It allows you to not incur sewer charges on activities like watering your lawn or filling your pool, because the water used is not returned to the sewer system. Savings depend on where you live, but in some cities, especially in warmer months, this could mean $40 to $100 per month in savings; call your water company to ask about your possible savings from this. *Average savings: $50 per year, though this depends on a lot of water usage and where you live.*

4. Use a Chimney Balloon

Even when you close the chimney flue, warm air escapes, which can cost some families upward of $100 a year. To fix that, buy what's called a chimney balloon—an inexpensive balloon made to block air from escaping from your chimney. It will pay for itself in under a year. *Average savings: $50 per year.*

5. Make One Phone Call, Save on Television

If you can't bring yourself to cut the cord—and in my house, my husband is a die-hard sports fan and claims to "need" premium channels for such things (you pick your battles in a marriage, and I'm leaving this one alone!)—you probably face a $100 TV bill each month. To lower it, find a better offer from a competitor, even if you have no intention of switching. Call your current provider with the competitor's offer in hand, and ask if they can they match it. Sometimes, even if they can't match that exact offer, they may have something else in the bag. Typically, cable providers' discount offers are good for about six months, and then the prices go up—they are banking on you forgetting this and simply paying more. So put a reminder on your calendar for that week to call the cable company again once the discounted rate is over. It's also worth asking if there is a big discount for bundling internet, cable, and phone, for example. Just read the fine print on these deals to make sure you really need all the things that come with the bundle.

If that doesn't work—and it is far from guaranteed these days as in many cities there isn't a ton of competition among television companies—Chris Voss, the former FBI lead international kidnapping negotiator (the man knows a thing or two about getting his way!) shared these tips with the team at Moneyish when we interviewed him for the video series "Everyday Hostages." He says that you should point out that you are a loyal customer and always pay on time, and that it seems like despite that loyalty the cable company is willing to give new customers, who aren't so loyal, a better deal. Then ask: "How am I supposed to live with that?" After that, "you will hear crickets from the person at the end of the line," he says. Then ask if there is anything they can do. If that doesn't work, say,

"Wow, it sounds like you are powerless here." Voss, who is the author of "Never Split the Difference: Negotiate As If Your Life Depended On It," says, "No one wants to say 'yes' to that...they will try to help you." And of course, during this whole exchange, be polite—even though that sometimes feels worse than childbirth! *Average savings: $10 to $20 a month.*

Quick Tip

If you're going on an extended vacation, some cable companies have something called a "vacation hold" where you can temporarily suspend service for a small fee. That can save you money!

---

6. Get All the Savings You Can on Your Cell Phone

At some point the whole family is on your cell phone plan and that can be insanely expensive. And there seems to be a new better-seeming deal tossed at you every month or so. To keep it simple, I love the *Consumer Reports* guide to low-cost cell phone plans; it's simple and helps you figure out which one might be right for you. Just remember to think about which service works best in your area. Beyond that, here are other ways to save.

First, make sure you're getting all the discounts: Students, military, teachers, and government workers can all save, as can many employees (I currently get 20 percent off my cell phone plan through work; check with HR to see if you might get a perk like this). You can also bundle your cell phone with your cable or internet, if applicable, to save. And, perhaps one of the most effective ways to save these days: Get on the phone. The competition between cell phone companies is fierce, so threatening to cancel—especially if you're a good customer who comes armed with a competitor's deal—can help you save each and every month. *Average savings: $10 per month.*

Home Sweet Home Insurance

Most standard homeowner's insurance policies cover four things: your home itself, what's inside it, liability (like if someone sues you, gets hurt in your home, or your pet bites them), and temporary living expenses should something happen to your home and you can't live in it. They do not cover damage from floods and earthquakes, however, so if you're in a place prone to those, you will need additional coverage. Make sure your policy covers these things:

Enough to entirely rebuild your home from the ground up.
The cost of rebuilding is complicated to figure out (usually experts say that you should contact a local builder and check online to figure it out), and it's not the same as your home's value (it could actually cost you more to rebuild your home than the home is worth, for example). This is why you might consider using an independent insurance agent to help out; they have experience in making these kinds of estimates.

For most people, extended replacement coverage—which typically pays out your home's value plus 20 to 25 percent more—and an inflation guard, which automatically increases the insured value of your home as inflation increases, are enough. Guaranteed replacement coverage is even more comprehensive but the policies are more expensive and increasingly harder to find.

Enough to refurnish and replace everything in your home.
Get replacement cost coverage (not actual cash value coverage) to make sure that you get enough money to actually replace

everything in your home. If you get actual cash value of the items, it will be much less thanks to depreciation. III.org and Bankrate.com can help you figure out how much coverage you need, or work with your independent insurance agent to determine this. You will need additional coverage if you have pricey jewelry, art, family heirlooms, et cetera.

If you rent: You want to look for the same thing (replacement cost coverage) in your renter's insurance policy (a must!).

Enough liability to cover all of your assets.

You want enough liability coverage to cover the total dollar amount of all of your assets (home, retirement funds, savings, jewelry, et cetera). Most policies cover between about $100,000 and $300,000; if your assets are worth more than that, you will need to purchase additional liability coverage.

So now that you know what you need, let's look at ways to make it more affordable.

1. Get a Lower Priced Homeowner's Insurance Policy

Homeowner's insurance is expensive—$1,186 per year, on average, according to J.D. Power in 2016—but you can often slash your rates by doing one of two things. First, you should be shopping around for better rates at least every couple of years; go on your state's insurance department website (a quick Google search will help you find this) and see if they publish sample rates from different companies. Pick three or four companies with decent rates that also have low complaint ratios (the number of complaints relative to how large their business is). Then call the best companies to get your rate, or use sites like Insure.com or Esurance.com. For fifteen years in a row now, Amica has ranked highest in terms of customer satisfaction, according to J.D. Power. If you don't feel like doing all this legwork, try my home insurance hack to tackle your homeowner's insurance in two and a half hours and save an estimated $300 this year. *Average savings: $300 per year.*

Home Insurance Hack

Don't feel like figuring out how much homeowner's insurance you need or calling around to get quotes? Use an independent insurance broker to shop around for you. These brokers don't work for one single insurance company, so they will look around for policies for you. They make a commission when they sell you the policy, but the commission is paid for by the insurance company, not you.

Step 1: Identify three independent brokers. If you can get a recommendation from someone that's usually best; if not, TrustedChoice.com will show you a list of independent agents in your area. Cross-reference the agency you're thinking of going with with Better Business Bureau ratings and Yelp reviews. Then call them to get a feel for which one might make the most sense for you. Make sure the agent asks a lot of questions about your home and your insurance needs.

Estimated time: 20 minutes per call, 1 hour total.

Step 2: Choose your policy. Have the agent you like give you quotes from three companies. Then have the agent go over each quote and what it covers with you. You, of course, still need to vet the policy yourself. Then pick the one that offers the best coverage for the lowest price.

Estimated time: 1½ hours.

Average savings: $300 per year.

2. Get All the Discounts You Can on Your Homeowner's Insurance Policy

One of the biggest ways to save (sometimes up to 30 percent off your total bill) is to get your car, life, and homeowner's insurance from the same company. A survey from InsuranceQuotes.com found that you can save an average of $314 per year by bundling your homeowner's insurance and auto insurance.

It's also worth calling your current insurance company when looking at other options. If your current provider thinks you might leave for another firm, they're often willing to cut you a deal. You should also ask about other discounts they can offer you. These often include discounts for people who haven't made any claims in years, who are longtime customers with the company, who live in a gated community or in a community with a homeowner's association, who don't smoke, who have high-quality alarm systems, or who install gas and water sensors (you can find these at Home Depot and Lowe's). It's a call that won't take more than 30 minutes, and can save you $100+ (and sometimes significantly more) this year. *Average savings: $100 per year.*

3. Raise Your Deductible

This sounds like a duh, but many people don't realize just how much they can save by raising their $500 deductible to something higher. Lower deductibles mean higher annual premiums, and raising your deductible can make sense as homeowner's insurance should only be used for large issues. Remember if you file too many small claims, the insurer will likely raise your rates so it often makes sense to raise your deductible, assuming, of course, that you have the savings to pay that deductible should you ever need it. But if you don't, we'll get to that in Chapter 15. Just keep in mind that unlike your health insurance, the deductible is not cumulative over the whole year, it will be applied to each claim.

Raise your deductible from $500 to:	Get a discount of:	For the average homeowner this means a savings of:
$1,000	8.51 percent	$72 per year
$2,000	15 percent	$126 per year

Source: InsuranceQuotes.com/Quadrant Information Services, 2016.

Get Smart about Home Repairs

Roughly half of Americans experience a major, unforeseen expense in a given year, according to data from American Express. Of those, about one in three were hit with a repair or needed upgrade on their home that they didn't expect. Often, these things can cost thousands, so it's important that you get a good deal and a contractor who does good work.

Here is a simple way to do this, though it will take some time. Use a contractor who comes recommended. If you don't know one, you can use HomeAdvisor.com, which vets contactors for licensing, criminal history, and more, or check reviews on Angie's List. You should also ask to see the contractor's work and talk to past clients. Next, get at least three quotes from different contractors. If someone comes in way cheaper than the others, it could be a red flag. Sometimes that person doesn't have a full understanding of the costs of the project or insufficient staff to help, or plans to pad that number once he starts the job with a lot of upselling or telling you you must fix things that he didn't see before. Ask him to explain his low cost. And, of course, make sure he is insured.

Once you've hired the person, try to restrict upfront payments to about 30 percent of the total cost (though with materials you may have to go a bit higher); then withhold the final payment for the job for thirty days so you can make sure the contractor did a good job.

How the Kellys Saved $7,300 a Year on Housing

In 2005, Cheri and Matt Kelly of Durango, Colorado, faced a situation that is all too familiar these days: a pile of debt. The couple owed roughly $65,000—a combination of credit cards (the bulk of it), student loans, and medical bills—and it was stressing them out. For years, they simply paid the minimums on their debts and ignored the problem; they barely even talked to one another about it. But one day (after briefly contemplating bankruptcy) they'd had enough. The couple decided to aggressively tackle their debt. They did some smaller things to cut spending: Hosting a garage sale that netted them about $1,500; slashing food costs from $500 to $300 per month by eating more chicken and less beef, making lots of soups and lasagnas, and just drinking water; and cutting their entertainment and extras budget down to just $30 per week for each family member. But the biggest thing they did was downsize their home. They had been living in a large condo (complete with a pool table in their son's room), and they sold it to move into a much smaller place. Their living costs went from $1,300 per month to $685 per month—which meant they had more than $7,300 a year extra.

"We don't miss the space—not even a little bit," Matt Kelly says. "Our large condo was three stories tall. We often found each of us on one floor, not interacting with anyone else. In our smaller condo, 863 square feet, we are in close proximity so interaction, spontaneous communication, is natural. Over time we have reframed what space is. There is so much public shared space in the world that we don't feel any sense of lack."

THE ONE THING

Do This and You Will Automatically Save Thousands for the Rest of Your Life

You must, must know your credit score, which is a three-digit number that tells a lender how likely it is that you will pay back what you borrow in full and on time. The number is calculated based on your past financial behavior, like whether you paid bills on time and how much debt you have (more on this later).

Pretty much every single company that loans you money (a car dealership, a bank, et cetera) will look at this number and use it to figure out what interest rate they will charge you on that loan. If your score isn't good they might not lend you the money at all, and if they do lend it to you, you'll have to pay a higher—sometimes much higher—interest rate to get it. That could cost you tens of thousands of dollars!

Let's look at an example. Let's say you get a thirty-year loan for $200,000 to buy a house at a fixed interest rate of 5 percent; you will pay more than $186,000 in interest (on top of the cost of the home) to borrow that money. Now let's say that, because of your credit score, you got that same loan at a 6 percent rate. You'd pay more than $230,000 in interest—$44,000 more than the person who got a 5 percent rate. So yes, this advice can literally save you tens of thousands of dollars.

How to Find Out Your Credit Score

You are entitled to one free credit report from each of the three credit bureaus (the companies that keep track of your credit score) every twelve months. To request it, go to AnnualCreditReport.com. Don't go to other sites to get it; these are often scams. Your reports on each one may be a little different due to errors and the fact that some companies don't report your past financial behavior to all credit bureaus. To get your actual scores for free, sign up on sites like WalletHub.com and CreditKarma.com.

What's a Good Score and How Do I Get One?

Scores range from 300 to 850. Aim for a score of 760 or higher. If you don't have one that is that high, first look for errors, such as a strange account that doesn't belong to you but appears on your report, or a late payment that you didn't actually pay late. Either of those things could be bringing down your score. Each credit bureau has a method for how you can dispute things on your report that you can find on their website. Next, you will need to change your behavior going forward so that it reflects well on your credit report. Here are five things you can do to boost your score:

Pay All Your Bills on Time

I recommend scheduling automatic bill pay for many of your bills so you never forget; at the very least, put a reminder to yourself on the calendar so you don't space out on these bills.

Don't Cancel Credit Cards You've Had for a Long Time

You don't need to use the cards, but canceling them can hurt your score.

Raise the Limit on the Credit Card You Do Have

Obviously, don't spend up to this limit, just raise the limit on paper! This sounds strange, I know, but part of your credit score is determined by the total amount of credit you have available to you.

Don't Apply for a Bunch of New Credit Cards or Loans at One Time

Lenders think of this as risky behavior, so it can drag down your score.

Pay Down Debts

If you have, say, a pile of credit card debt, paying it off will help your score.

Chapter 4

Clothing
Dress for Less

Believe me, I get wanting to dress your child in head-to-toe Gap Kids—especially while they're young and aren't yet fighting you to only wear *Frozen* or *Power Rangers* everything! But, as my mom always says to me, life happens. And life, with kids, involves food stains, dirt smears, rips, tears, and growing out of things so quickly that you wonder what the heck the kid is eating when you're not around. That means that us moms have to try to resist the urge to drop big bucks on clothes. Now, I'm not going to go crazy with tips in this chapter, as you probably know how to get great clothing deals, but I did want to share what I've found to be especially helpful.

1. Get in on the Mommy Marketplace

Buying things used is obviously a great way to save. To do it, you should shop local Listservs and Facebook groups. If you aren't sure if there is a mom's group in your town, ask your fellow moms or do a quick Google or Facebook search with your town's name and "mom's group" or similar words. Then, join mommy Listservs and groups for ALL the neighborhoods near (and sort of near) you. It's usually simple to join; on Facebook, for example, you find the group and then just send them a request to become a member. This is the number one way I've saved money on clothes and toys for my daughter—not only did I join the mommy Listservs and Facebook groups in my neighborhood, I also joined a ton of others in the posh neighborhoods nearby. I admit I loved reading other moms' concerns anyway—it made me feel like I was doing an okay job as a parent, yahoo!—and then I'd also see stuff I needed for sale, win-win! And let me tell you: Mommies give away awesome stuff! You can snag piles of adorbs clothes—in addition to boxes of unused diapers, toys, bouncy chairs, swings, and strollers—for next to nothing and sometimes free. Let's be serious, this is way better than Craigslist, which can be, well, creepy sometimes. You should also definitely use these groups to organize clothing swaps for you (because let's face it, your former clothes may never fit the same again!) and for the kids. Don't get things like cribs or car seats on these groups, however, because you don't know what happened to them in the past, and this could present safety issues.

Put Too-Small Disposable Diapers to Good Use

Pretty much every mom I know has bought a huge pack of diapers in one size and midway through the box, their kid has a growth spurt—and needs the next size up. First, you need to know the weight limits on diapers are often BS—off by a pound or two. Larger diapers cost slightly more, so the companies want you to size up quickly. But don't fall for their trick and toss diapers just because the box says your kid is now too heavy for them.

If your baby really does need a larger size, there are a few things you can do with those too-small diapers (and yes, they're a little weird but no one ever has to know you did this!).

The easiest thing is to use them as padding. If you want to store china or something breakable, use those diapers to separate the breakable items rather than having to buy a bunch of bubble wrap. You can also use them to clean things like big spills. I once used one on my Swiffer when I was in a pinch, no joke. And those diapers can keep you from having to buy more plants because you forgot to water them. Just put the diaper in the bottom of the pot before you pot the plant. The diaper will keep water from running out so the plant stays moist.

If you have a large quantity of unused diapers, google where to donate them in your city—there are tons of less fortunate parents who have trouble affording diapers.

2. Shop Secondhand Clothing Stores Smartly

If you want to buy cute kids clothes on the cheap, secondhand is the way to go. You probably already get a ton of free hand-me-downs from friends and family (A+ for you, as that's the best way to slash your costs), but for all of those clothes you still need in spite of that, save by getting smart about buying secondhand.

First check out thredUP.com, if you haven't already, for used kids clothes—super cute stuff and it's way easier to search and use than eBay, which also has good deals.

If you've been eyeing something adorbs in a secondhand shop near you, but still don't want to pay their asking price, here's a secret: Many stores consign on thirty-, sixty-, and ninety-day schedules. So after thirty days, a piece of merchandise may be marked down by roughly 20 to 25 percent and after sixty days by about 50 percent.

This varies somewhat from store to store, but stores will tell you their policy if you ask—just imply you want to know so you can sell them your kids' old clothes. This will help you figure out when the item you want will go on sale (and you can bury it on the rack and hope no one else gets it before you do).

3. Beware the "Pink Tax" on Your Daughter

Many items, particularly clothes, marketed to girls are more expensive than very similar items marketed to boys. Basically, they make it pink and mark it way the heck up, despite the products being nearly identical. On average, girls' clothing costs 4 percent more than boys' clothing. In some categories, the discrepancy was even larger—girls' children-size shirts are 13 percent more; children size jeans 8 percent more; and baby pants 9 percent more. Toys marketed to girls are, on average, 7 percent more expensive than boys' toys, according to an examination of nearly eight hundred products from ninety brands. Out of the fifteen clothing and toy categories surveyed, none of the toys cost less for girls, and only children's underwear and shoes cost less (at –3 percent) for girls than boys.

Whether it's more expensive to raise a son or a daughter is up for debate—some researchers and parents swear girls cost more (the pink tax being a big reason why), others swear boys do. For example, some say boys put more wear and tear on items, so you replace them more often. Seems like a bit of a stereotype to me, but hey, just repeating theories! And while girls face the pink tax, they're also less likely than boys to move home after college or to ask for financial help from you after college, so that's a big plus!

Still, there's little doubt that clothing, toys, and other goodies marketed to girls will cost you more over the years. The solution to the pink tax is boring and, as it happens, very in right now: Go for neutrals. When they're really little and haven't yet experienced the "it must have a princess on it" mentality, you can get away with this without a total meltdown ensuing, so take advantage while you can! When it comes to clothing, you can easily buy the plain tees and socks in the boys section and nobody's going to know the difference.

4. Know When Clothing Goes on Sale

Dreaming of an amazing jacket or something else cool for your little one but can't afford it at full price? The best timing for a shopping trip is often about six to eight weeks after the item you want has hit stores; once an item has lingered in the store for six weeks or more, the retailer is likely to mark it down to try to sell it, so check back then for a new (and lower!) price.

But here's the real trick to getting deals: You have to wait until the season is in full swing (and especially toward the end of the season) to buy things. So, if you need a winter coat for your little one and can wait until after the new year to buy it, that's going to give you deals. Of course, this isn't always possible, which is why I'm always looking for clothes that can take me deeper into a new season. So for fall sales, I might look for an item that can work in winter, too (like a cute little skirt for my daughter that she can also wear with either light tights or thick leggings). Think about how things can layer and de-layer into different seasons. That might be able to help you hold out for seasonal sales! And don't neglect shopping the sales now for something you know the kids will need next year. I mean, I can't promise you they'll like it next year, but that's a whole different conversation....

Quick Tip

Try this gummy life hack: Has gum gotten stuck to your kid's clothes and you've had to toss them? You don't have to—freeze the garment; that will make the gum easier to get off it.

---

5. Know the Price-Adjustment Policy

Some stores will give you a onetime price adjustment, which means that they'll refund you the difference between the price you paid for the clothes and the sale price of the item. As of the writing of this book, Old Navy and the Gap offer a onetime price adjustment if an item is marked down within fourteen days of the date on your purchase.

Don't feel like having to track this? I use an app called Paribus that does it for you; you link the app to your email and they automatically track what you bought at stores like Old Navy, Gap, and Kohl's, and if a price adjustment happens, they will refund you the money automatically.

6. Know Where to Shop

As I said before, thredUP—and its under-$10 section in particular—are worth a look, though I know many moms love new clothes, too. Here's what I've learned about that: Though Amazon does have amazing deals on many things, clothing—at least as of now—often isn't one of them. Instead, opt for places like Kohl's, Target, Walmart, and T.J.Maxx—all of which tend to have way better prices and selection. You can also find some pretty amazing deals at Old Navy and the Gap if you wait for their coupons and sales. Personally, I'm a big fan of Old Navy clothing and when I find a sale I jump on it—especially if I think about how I can extend the use of the clothes. For example, a few years back, I bought an on-sale dress for my then one-year-old daughter at Old Navy for around $10; one year later, she wore it as a top with leggings under it.

7. Borrow Onetime-Use Clothing

Kids grow out of things fast! And that's why I think texting or using Facebook to ask friends with kids to borrow things that your kid will wear once is a great idea. If you have a wedding or a church event that you need a nice dress and shoes for, ask friends and family if anyone has something you can borrow for your daughter or son. This can easily save you $15 to $30 or more, depending on what you had to buy.

The Mom's Guide to Avoiding the Dry Cleaner

While I know you don't generally send your kid's clothes to the dry cleaner, it's still expensive to send your own there, so I'm going to tackle the topic anyway! Working couples can easily drop $500 or more a year just on dry cleaning, especially if you're like me and can't seem to avoid getting the kids' breakfast on your outfit every morning (I swear oatmeal has a magnetic attraction to silk!). Even worse: Studies show that women get charged more for dry cleaning than men. The average price to clean a man's shirt is nearly half what it is for a woman's shirt. Men pay an average of $2.06, while women pay $3.95—and that's before you add in the extra cost for certain fabrics like silk or embellishments like sequins.

But not every garment that says dry-clean only has to be only dry-cleaned. You can typically hand wash items made from cotton, linen, and silk at home in cold water in your sink using a mild detergent like Woolite, rather than send them to the dry cleaner. Do a spot test on the item ahead of plopping it in the water just to make sure it looks okay. However, leave the rayon, wool, and cashmere to the dry cleaner, as well as things like suits or items with a lot of embellishments or pleats.

Momsanity Advice

Q: How can I get over the envy I feel when I see what other moms can and do buy for their kids that I can't afford?

A: Everyone covets things others have sometimes. I mean, I would love to be a mom with Pilates-toned abs who could wear white without staining it in five minutes, but it's not gonna happen. But if you can't get your jealousies out of your head, it's time to examine what's going on. Elizabeth Lombardo, author of *Better than Perfect: 7 Strategies to Crush Your Inner Critic and Create a Life You Love,* says you need to ask yourself, "What would be different in my life if I had whatever that mom has?"—be it a cool new stroller, a fancy new tennis racket or violin for your kid, or a barre booty. Most likely, nothing significant would happen. It wouldn't change what's important to your happiness, like your relationship with your family. And that's how you know this thing she has and you don't isn't really all that important. "If we base our self-worth on conditions, we will never be satisfied," she says. She's right. If we go around thinking: If I had a nicer house or a better car, then I'd be happy—*then* we're never going to be happy. She told me about an affluent woman she knew who was devastated because a friend had bought a private jet bigger than the one she had. Yes, there will always be someone richer, and always someone who wants to throw their money in your face. So when the green envy monster rears its ugly head (and it will!) you have to take a step back. Spend ten minutes or so writing down all the things that are great about your life: amazing kids, a kind spouse, a decent job. Keep that list somewhere accessible; refer to it; cherish it.

Chapter 5

Childcare
*Picking and Paying for
Daycare and Babysitters*

If there's one thing every new mom needs (besides twenty-four straight hours of sleep and a stiff martini come 8 p.m.), it's time away from the kids. You love 'em, but they're exhausting! I mean, there are some days when it's only 9 a.m. in my house, and my husband and I look at each other like: *How are we going to make it through this day, and where might we find a last-minute babysitter who doesn't charge a fortune?* Don't get me wrong, I love my little girl more than anything in the world, but there are days when she could win the whine Olympics, which means Mommy is more than willing to spend a little more than she should for a sitter.

And frankly, that expense is nothing compared to the shock many moms come face-to-face with when they get a daycare bill, which can average more than $11,000 a year. By the time they're ready for preschool, you could have bought you *and* the hubs a brand-new car for what you've paid!

Take Kristin Farrell, a single mom to an adorable toddler, who had to leave her full-time public relations job after her daughter was born because the hours and demands of that job weren't conducive to raising a child. She now works from home to spend more time with her daughter, but took a pay hit to do it. To save money, she has her daughter in daycare part-time (three days a week, at $140 a week) and on the other two days her mom watches her daughter. But "those days are rough," she says—her mom is older, "so a nine plus-hour day with a baby two days a week is too much." That means that on the days her mom is watching her daughter, Farrell often has to work and help take care of her little girl. "What typically happens is I squeeze in the time to work early in the morning and late at night to make up for the lost hours in the day," she says. "I'm very blessed to have the help I do and that I have a job that allows me to work from home," she says. "But honestly, some months I just have to gamble and hope the checks don't clear before I have money in the bank. Either that or put off credit card bills and take the hit there." Still, "it's all worth it," she says. "She gives me so much joy."

Daycare isn't the only crazily expensive childcare cost families face: A much-needed date night with your hubby can easily cost $100 between the babysitter ($10 an hour) and a meal out at a restaurant with a (CRUCIAL!) glass or two of wine. Do that just once a month, and you're facing $1,200 or more a year in extra expenses.

So what's a mom to do? This chapter will help you figure out how much you might spend on childcare and how to go about paying for it.

Babysitters

Let's start with the babysitters. Until I researched this topic, I was constantly wondering if I was paying my babysitter too much. I mean, she'd come after my daughter was asleep, watch a few hours of *Dateline* while snacking on a tub of popcorn, and end up making enough for a nice dinner out with her boyfriend. Then again, she was safeguarding the most precious thing in my life: my daughter. So I did a little homework, and here's what I found.

Babysitter pay ranges from about $7.50 per hour on the very low end to more than $15 per hour on the high end, according to data from PayScale.com; the average nationwide is about $10 per hour. Typically if you live in a rural area or a fairly inexpensive city (these tend to be in the South and middle of the country), you'll fall on the low end of this spectrum. Those who live on the coasts or in large, pricey cities tend to pay more.

Below is a breakdown by major U.S. cities. The averages in the table didn't take into account number of children, but you can assume in many cases that the parents had more than one child, which may skew the numbers higher. So don't worry if you pay a little less than these numbers. If you don't see your city on the list, you can use the Babysitting Rates Calculator on Care.com to get the average for your area; I find that these rates—as well as the rates in the chart—are sometimes a bit high but still a good starting point for figuring out what to pay. You can also ask local moms what they pay their sitters to get an idea.

As a general rule of thumb, if you have another child, you should pay your babysitter more to watch them both (typically an extra $1 to $2 per hour). Also, if you want a sitter who is very experienced and/or CPR or first-aid trained, who does a lot of extras like cook and clean, or who travels a long way to get to you, expect to pay about $1 per hour more for her, too. And, of course, if you're going to be out later than you said you would be, text her as soon as possible to let her know, and pay her for that extra time plus a little extra.

What Babysitters Make per Hour by City

Akron, OH	$12.67	Harrisburg, VA	$12.67	Philadelphia, PA	$14.02
Albany, NY	$13.81	Hartford, CT	$14.28	Phoenix, AZ	$13.48
Albuquerque, NM	$13.22	Honolulu, HI	$13.13	Pittsburgh, PA	$13.66
Atlanta, GA	$13.75	Houston, TX	$13.76	Portland, OR	$13.98
Augusta, GA	$12.70	Indianapolis, IN	$12.32	Providence, RI	$13.98
Austin, TX	$14.17	Jacksonville, FL	$12.75	Raleigh, NC	$13.40
Baltimore, MD	$13.99	Kansas City, KS/MO	$12.61	Richmond, VA	$13.41
Boise, ID	$13.28	Las Vegas, NV	$13.47	Riverside, CA	$13.58
Boston, MA	$15.51	Little Rock, AR	$12.31	Rochester, NY	$13.29
Charleston, SC	$13.85	Los Angeles, CA	$14.27	Sacramento, CA	$14.42
Charlotte, NC	$13.50	Louisville, KY	$12.50	Salt Lake City, UT	$13.21
Chicago, IL	$13.93	Madison, WI	$12.86	San Antonio, TX	$13.20
Cincinnati, OH	$13.36	Memphis, TN	$12.94	San Diego, CA	$14.26
Colorado Springs, CO	$13.11	Miami, FL	$13.48	San Francisco, CA	$16.52

(Continued)

City	Rate	City	Rate	City	Rate
Columbia, SC	$13.18	Milwaukee, WI	$12.16	San Jose, CA	$16.68
Columbus, OH	$13.15	Minneapolis, MN	$12.99	Sarasota, FL	$13.35
Dallas, TX	$13.65	Nashville, TN	$13.50	Seattle, WA	$14.95
Denver, CO	$14.06	New Orleans, LA	$13.70	St. Louis, MO	$13.39
Des Moines, IA	$13.20	New York, NY	$15.09	Tampa, FL	$13.27
Detroit, MI	$13.12	Oklahoma City, OK	$13.01	Tucson, AZ	$13.06
Fort Myers, FL	$13.76	Omaha, NE	$12.16	Tulsa, OK	$12.86
Grand Rapids, MI	$12.81	Orlando, FL	$12.57	Washington, D.C.	$14.92

Source: Care.com, 2016.

How to Save on Babysitting (Without Sacrificing Quality)

One of the best ways to save on babysitting is to organize a babysitting co-op with other area parents—you babysit for their kids, they babysit for yours. You can do this with your small group of friends or use a local Facebook moms group to get this started on a larger level. You can also coordinate with other parents to get one babysitter for a group of kids for a date night; that can cut the price of the sitter in half or more for each parent. It's also worth considering a "mother's helper"—a much younger kid (say eleven to thirteen) to watch your kid just so you can get things done at home. You'll be there pseudo supervising them, but don't have to entertain your child the whole time. Also check your local gym, YMCA, or parks department; some offer super low-cost classes for children and adults and other free childcare. That can be a savior!

Where to Find Good Babysitters

In most cases, the best place to find a sitter is by asking friends and family or seeing if someone from your child's daycare is available to babysit. If your child isn't in daycare, but a friend's kid is, ask them if they can ask their daycare workers if they want some extra money babysitting. If that doesn't yield results, go deeper into your social network—that coworker you've taken a shine to or the woman in your yoga class who's always chatting with her kids on the phone before class. Or try one of these sites—Care.com, UrbanSitter.com, or Sittercity.com—all of which offer reviewed sitters typically for a monthly fee.

Vetting the Babysitter

Whether or not a babysitter comes to you via a personal reference, it's always a good idea to meet and interview her yourself.

Ask:

1. **The basics:** Name, address, age, and phone number, as well as hourly rate and typical availability.
2. **General:** What she likes about babysitting—and what she finds most challenging.
3. **Experience:** How often she babysits and what ages of kids she has experience with.
4. **Activities:** What she typically does to entertain the kids.
5. **Difficult situations:** How she handles it when kids are upset, and how she deals when they misbehave. Ask her about her hardest babysitting moment and how she handled it. Ask if she's had a problem with any parents who hired her, or in following their wishes, and how she handled that. Finally, ask if she's had an emergency while babysitting, and if so what she did.
6. **Certifications:** If she is first-aid or CPR-trained. If not, would she be willing to get it.
7. **Personal questions:** It's important to ask her questions about herself—what she likes to do in her free time, what she's studying in school, et cetera.
8. **Other considerations:** If you're going to want her to cook for or bathe kids or take them on outings, you should ask her if she is okay with doing things like this and how she would handle it.
9. **Three references:** Names, when she worked for them, phone number, and email.

10. **Conclude:** Ask her if she has questions for you to encourage more conversation.

11. **Follow up:** After the interview, call the people she gave as references. Ask them about her strengths, weaknesses, how long she worked for them (and why she no longer does, if that's true), and their overall impression of her. Then dig a bit into exactly who she is by looking through her social media (Facebook, Instagram, Twitter, Snapchat, et cetera); you can get a good sense of a person from what they post online. The sitter may seem nice, but her photos could feature a few too many red Solo cups for your liking. Finally, consider doing a background check. You can use a company like Intelius, US Search, or Inforegistry to do it, but remember: These aren't always perfect and sometimes contain false information.

What Summer Camp Will Cost You

Ohhh the joys of a silent house! But ohhh the price for making that happen—or at least for some camps! Seriously, the prices vary from less than $100 to $1,500 a week or more, according to the American Camp Association. About one in five families now spend $2,000 or more to send their child to summer camp, according to Care.com. Don't freak out about this yet, though; in Chapter 19, I'm going to show you how to save for something like this.

Daycare 101

The single biggest shock to me when I became a mom (other than the fact that my daughter literally colic-cried for four hours a night every night for her first two months of life) was the cost of daycare. Seriously, around where I live there were places asking $2,400 a month; um, excuse me, I am a writer, how do you think I am going to swing that? And even the cheaper places were still $1,700 a month. I had a panic attack in the street one day wondering how my husband and I would afford that (in case you're wondering, it really does feel like a heart attack) and still manage to save for retirement and pay our mortgage.

I'm not exaggerating this cost: In roughly half the states in this country, full-time daycare now costs more than a full year of tuition at a public, in-state college. Yes, there you were worrying about how you'd afford college when the real threat to your financial future is getting someone to watch your toddler scribble crayon on the wall and try his best not to learn to count to ten. Across the nation, the average cost of daycare is about $9,500 per year—and residents of some cities have it way worse! We eventually found a solution that worked for us by doing a nanny share with our next-door neighbors to save money. But I know many moms don't have that option. So I'll give you some tips on how you can save on daycare.

What It Costs to Send Your Child to Daycare Each Year

If you don't see your city listed on this chart—and many aren't—check Care.com's Care Index. While they don't have in-center daycare costs for all cities, they do list more than are included in this chart.

Albany, NY	$10,990
Albuquerque, NM	$9,527
Allentown, PA	$8,264
Atlanta, GA	$9,374
Austin, TX	$10,561
Baltimore, MD	$10,642

Baton Rouge, LA	$7,116
Boise, ID	$8,094
Boston, MA	$14,960
Buffalo, NY	$11,239
Cedar Rapids, IA	$8,781
Charleston, SC	$8,448
Charlotte, NC	$10,670
Chicago, IL	$11,323
Cincinnati, OH	$8,832
Cleveland, OH	$9,317
Columbus, OH	$9,363
Dallas, TX	$9,004
Dayton, OH	$8,298
Denver, CO	$11,578
Des Moines, IA	$9,658
Detroit, MI	$9,759
Durham, NC	$12,050
Erie, PA	$8,584
Grand Rapids, MI	$8,510
Greensboro, NC	$7,656
Harrisburg, PA	$9,055
Hartford, CT	$11,180
Honolulu, HI	$12,040
Houston, TX	$8,439

(*Continued*)

Hyannis, MA	$12,029
Indianapolis, IN	$8,567
Iowa City, IA	$9,466
Jacksonville, FL	$8,729
Kansas City, KS/MO	$8,751
Knoxville, TN	$8,104
Lancaster, PA	$9,275
Las Vegas, NV	$9,723
Lincoln, NE	$8,590
Little Rock, AR	$6,322
Los Angeles, CA	$11,611
Louisville, KY	$8,728
Madison, WI	$11,842
Memphis, TN	$7,467
Miami, FL	$9,166
Milwaukee, WI	$11,608
Minneapolis, MN	$11,064
Nashville, TN	$8,251
New Haven, CT	$12,140
New Orleans, LA	$7,554
New York, NY	$12,167
Norfolk, VA	$7,853
Oklahoma City, OK	$8,053
Omaha, NE	$8,522
Orlando, FL	$8,446

Oxnard, CA	$11,190
Philadelphia, PA	$10,176
Phoenix, AZ	$8,995
Pittsburgh, PA	$9,136
Portland, ME	$9,590
Portland, OR	$11,504
Providence, RI	$11,106
Raleigh, NC	$9,419
Reading, PA	$8,950
Richmond, VA	$8,465
Riverside, CA	$8,964
Rochester, NY	$9,757
Sacramento, CA	$10,453
Salt Lake City, UT	$8,618
San Antonio, TX	$8,498
San Diego, CA	$11,115
San Francisco, CA	$15,481
San Jose, CA	$15,177
Santa Rosa, CA	$12,130
Scranton, PA	$7,664
Seattle, WA	$12,624
Sioux City, IA	$7,948
Springfield, MO	$11,577
St. Louis, MO	$8,961

(Continued)

Stamford, CT	$15,147
Stockton, CA	$8,869
Syracuse, NY	$9,527
Tampa, FL	$8,249
Tulsa, OK	$8,440
Washington, D.C.	$12,058
Worcester, MA	$12,146

Source: Care.com, 2016.

Finding a Good Daycare

If you have to work full-time like me, your child will spend nearly as much time at his daycare center as he does with you—which makes it essential you pick the right one (but also one you can afford). To start your search, ask fellow parents. If you don't know anyone with a child in daycare, ask moms you meet at the playground, your pediatrician, moms on your mommy Listserv, and Facebook groups for recommendations.

Once you have a few promising leads, call the daycare centers to get the basics:

1. **Cost:** If this comes in too high, ask about discounts if you decide to go with this daycare (see page 79).
2. **Hours:** What are the center's regular hours and what happens when parents are late?
3. **Start date:** When can your child start attending? Sometimes daycare centers have waiting lists, which makes it important to start searching for a center a least a couple months before you'll actually need to use it.
4. **Accreditation:** Each state has different licensing requirements

for daycare (you can read more about this at ChildCare
Aware.org). Center-based daycares that are accredited by
the National Association for the Education of Young Children (NAEYC.org) and home-based daycares accredited by
the National Association of Family Child Care (NAFCC.org)
may have higher standards of care because they have to meet
certain guidelines. While accreditations likes these aren't a
"must" (plenty of home-based daycares, for example, are lov-
ing and wonderful and don't have accreditation), it does hint
to you that the daycare follows certain standards of care.

5. **Routine:** What is a typical day for your child at the center? If
    you like what you hear over the phone, go in for a visit and ask
    the questions listed below.

6. **References:** Finally, if a center seems like the one you want,
    ask them for contact information of parents who send their
    child there. Call these parents and ask about their experience.
    Also post about the daycare on Listservs and groups asking
    other moms about it, which will give you the most unbiased
    feedback on the daycare.

Two Surprising Signs of a Less-than-Stellar Daycare

1. **It's too clean.** While a super clean room, on its face, is likely
    to wow parents, it may be a bad sign. A room that is too clean
    after a full day of daycare often shows that the kids aren't
    allowed to fully explore and play, and that instead daycare
    providers are more concerned with appearance than actual
    experience for the kids.

2. **It doesn't allow unannounced visits.** The center may say that
    this is a safety measure, but if they don't allow unannounced
    visits from parents, this can be a sign that how the daycare really
    operates versus what they show you on the tour don't match up.

What to Look for When Visiting a Potential Daycare

Before you make your choice official, make an unannounced visit to see what the place is like when they're not fully prepared for you. When you visit—in addition to a happy and clean environment, where both the children and caregivers seem to enjoy themselves— here's what you should ask and look for:

1. **Caregiver to kid ratio:** Make sure that there are enough caregivers. In a center-based daycare, there should be a minimum of one staffer to every three infants, one staffer for every four young toddlers, and one staffer for every six to eight older toddlers/kids. For an in-home daycare, there shouldn't be more than about six total kids, and make sure that there aren't more than two infants in that mix.

2. **Discipline:** Ask them questions such as:
   - How would you handle it if my child hit another kid or another kid hit my child?
   - How do you handle it when you tell a child no and they continue the bad behavior?
   - How do you punish a misbehaving child?
   - How do you handle children that don't share?

Basically, you want to think of likely scenarios and ask about how they would treat it.

3. **Food:** What do you feed the kids and how do you handle it when kids don't eat? How do you handle allergies and other food sensitivities?

4. **Caregiver qualifications:** What kinds of certifications do caregivers have (CPR, first-aid trained, et cetera) and what

kind of experience do they have (childhood education/development classes, et cetera)?

5. **Parent involvement:** Ask how you can be involved in the center and if this is required. Are there activities for families, for example? You may be too busy with work to do this so it's important to know what is expected.

6. **Health:** What are their policies around sick kids and caregivers, and immunizations?

7. **Staff turnover:** How long has each staff member been with the center? High turnover is a bad sign.

8. **Background checks:** How have the caregivers been screened? Did they do a criminal and health background check?

9. **Environment:** Make sure the place has enough space, offers plenty of age-appropriate toys, and that kids have their own cribs or cots to nap on.

10. **Activities:** Look for a place where there is a range of activities from the educational to free play. It's also important that the kids of different ages have age-appropriate activities.

11. **Safety and security:** Make sure doors into and out of the center stay locked all day and that the center has smoke and carbon monoxide detectors. Make sure toys aren't choking hazards or easily breakable; that they have child gates in front of stairs and other dangers, and window guards so that kids can't climb out. Check that infants are put to sleep on their backs without blankets. Make sure areas are kept relatively clear of clutter so kids can't trip and get hurt.

12. **Cleanliness:** Changing areas should be very clean with areas to throw out diapers. Caregivers should wash their hands after changing diapers. The area where the children are, as well as kitchens and bathrooms should be clean.

13. **Other considerations:** For home-based care, you'll want to

know if the caregiver's insurance covers your kid, if other people and pets will be around (and if so, who they are and how often they will be around), and how the caregiver handles it if she has to take time off.

THE ONE THING

If You Only Do One Thing to Save on Childcare This Year, Do This

Use your dependent care FSA, if you're lucky enough to get one from your company (call HR to discuss this), which lets you save pretax money to pay for your childcare. You can save up to $5,000 for a married couple.

WageWorks.com has an excellent calculator that can show you, based on your individual income and tax rate, how much you can save by using a dependent care FSA. But let's look at an example of how this works. Let's assume you and your hubs make $60,000 a year, and have a tax rate of 30 percent. Without a dependent care FSA, you're paying $18,000 in taxes ($60,000 × 0.30 = $18,000). And then you're paying $5,000 (or more) of your take-home pay for daycare. But if you contribute the maximum $5,000 to your FSA account for childcare, that $5,000 is taken out of your income before taxes. So your taxes would be $55,000 × 0.30 = $16,500. You're still paying $5,000 for daycare, but you've saved $1,500 by reducing your taxable income.[2]

Bonus: You can also use this money to help pay for preschool and summer camp.

---

[2] Source: Adapted from WageWorks.com chart.

Set Up Your FSA in 30 Minutes or Less

You can typically only sign up for your dependent care FSA during your company's open enrollment period (these are typically in November), but it won't take you much time at all to contribute to it. Your company will typically offer you a menu of options during open enrollment with a dependent care FSA among them. If you see this option, it will typically take you less than fifteen minutes to select it and select how much to contribute to it. The dependent care FSA has rules (you can find them on the IRS website), including that the care must be for a child under thirteen; often you submit receipts for the care provided and are reimbursed for it.

The main question to ask yourself is: How much will you spend on childcare (including preschool, summer day camp, before/after school programs, daycare) in the coming year? Be conservative, as this is a use-it-or-lose-it plan in which if you don't use the money it doesn't roll into the next year. Then elect to fund that much into the account. The money is automatically deducted from your pay before taxes are taken out.

Call HR if you have any questions about how this works, how payments are made, et cetera.

Ten Simple Ways to Save on Daycare

You don't want to skimp on quality, obviously, but there are many ways to save beyond the dependent care FSA.

1. Ask the daycare about these discounts (which are often available but not advertised):
   o **Referrals:** Many daycares will give you a sizeable credit if you refer another family to them.

○ **Siblings:** If you send your second child to the same daycare, they may go at a discounted rate.

○ **Prepayment:** If you pay months in advance, you may get a break on your total bill.

If those don't work, simply ask them how you can save.

2. Barter with the daycare. Daycare owners likely need help with things like bookkeeping, accounting, and cleaning. If you have skills like that, see if you can barter for a lower rate; you'll want to approach the owner about this.

3. Ask your company (HR will know) what discounts it offers. Some offer discounts at certain daycares, backup childcare cash, and more.

4. When you file your taxes, take the Child and Dependent Care Tax Credit if you're eligible. This gives you a tax credit of up to 35 percent on $3,000 worth of childcare related expenses for one child or dependent, or up to $6,000 for two or more children. So, let's say you qualify for the 35 percent credit and you had $4,000 in childcare expenses; you might get a $1,400 credit (that's 35 percent of $4,000). If you file your taxes online, the software usually walks you through your eligibility for this. If you use an accountant, just be sure to mention this.

5. Look into home-based or church-based daycares, which can be cheaper. Just do your homework on them and talk to a number of other parents who have sent their children there.

6. See if there is a daycare co-op in your area, in which parents, on a rotating schedule, are the ones who take care of the kids. This gives everyone a discounted rate—you pay for things like shared toys, meals, et cetera, but labor is free since you and your fellow parents are doing it. If there isn't a co-op near you—and you're in a super-motivated mommy mode—see if you can create one. This won't work well for a nine-to-five

mom most likely, but a part-time working mom could benefit greatly from this. Care.com has resources on how to do this.

7. Start your daycare hunt early. Sometimes the more affordable ones fill faster.

8. See if your boss and/or your partner's boss will let you adjust your hours. You could go in earlier in the morning and leave early, your partner could go in later in the morning and stay later or vice versa. Even doing this for a couple days a week can save you a couple hundred bucks off the cost of daycare.

9. Consider a nanny share. Most people think "nanny" and think "too expensive" but this isn't necessarily true if you share one. My husband and I do a nanny share with our next-door neighbors, who have a son the same age as my daughter, and it saves us money over many of the area daycares. I found the nanny on one of my mommy Listservs, called her references and vetted her, and it couldn't have worked out better.

10. Cut other expenses. Even if you try all the above tricks, daycare may still seem astronomically expensive to you. That's why I wrote Chapters 2–4—they've got tons of tips that can save you hundreds of dollars each year; you can put that extra money into daycare.

Chapter 6

Transportation
Driving Toward Savings

I'm guessing you've gotten over your dreams of a fancy two-seater convertible—at least until the kids head off to college. And you may have even embraced your budget-friendly mom mobile. I mean, there is something about easily getting the kids into and out of their car seats that makes you feel like a superhero—even when you're driving something that looks eerily similar to a minivan. But there are plenty of savings you may still be missing when it comes to your car.

An easy way, of course, to slash your transportation costs is to buy a relatively inexpensive, reliable car that gets great gas mileage. Strongly consider buying it gently used because new cars lose roughly 20 percent of their value as soon as you drive them off the lot. After the first year, the car's value still goes down but not as rapidly. The used model—if you do your homework on it by checking its history on Carfax.com and getting a certified mechanic to look it over before you buy—will be almost as good as the new, but cost you an average of about $2,500 less.

By now, you've gotten plenty of negotiation practice trying to reason with a toddler over those four pieces of broccoli, and you must put it to good use. I know you know this, but the reality is that most people don't do it. Before you even set foot on the lot, do your homework. Use KBB.com or Edmunds.com to research car prices, so you come into the deal with what you think is a fair price. Kiplinger.com has a thorough piece called "How to Get the Best Deal on a Used Car" that is worth reading—it can be your bible for car buying. When you get to the lot, don't let the car dealer charge you too much. In a *Consumer Reports* survey, when people negotiated the price of a used car they ended up paying $900 on average less for the car than those who didn't negotiate. The strategy that worked best: simply asking for a lower price.

THE ONE THING

If You Only Do One Thing to Cut Car Costs, Do This

You can cut your annual transportation costs by an average of $356 per year (and for some, significantly more) by shopping around for your car insurance, a 2016 J.D. Power study found. One in three drivers say they never shop around for car insurance and another 30 percent say they only do it every few years, data from InsuranceQuotes.com shows. You should be doing this every year or so. Start by getting at least four quotes from different companies that have low complaint ratios (you can check this on the National Association of Insurance Commissioners website) and see which yields you the most savings for the best plan. I like NerdWallet's compare auto insurance tool—you fill out a short questionnaire and they list estimated quotes. I then double-check the companies from which they give quotes with the NAIC website for complaints. Seriously, the whole process will take you maybe two hours and you save an average of $356 per year—that's totally worth it!

Car Insurance 101

Your car insurance policy is actually a collection of different types of coverage, including:

1. **Bodily injury:** Covers medical costs if someone gets hurt in an accident that's your fault.
2. **Property damage liability:** Covers damage to other cars or property in an accident that's your fault.
3. **Collision:** Covers repairs to your car after an accident.
4. **Uninsured/underinsured motorists:** Covers costs if you get hit by an uninsured driver.
5. **Personal injury protection:** Covers your medical costs and possibly lost wages after an accident.
6. **Comprehensive:** Covers costs if your car is damaged in some way other than an accident, like theft or fire.

How Much Car Insurance Do You Need?

Most states have required minimum amounts of insurance, but many people need more than that. In the simplest of terms, you're going to want enough insurance to cover the value of all your assets (home, savings, jewelry, et cetera) should you get into an accident. Insurance.com has an easy calculator to help you get started figuring out how much insurance you need (it's under their "Auto" tab). Just remember that if the value of all of your assets exceeds the max level of protection they suggest for you, you're going to want to increase it to protect yourself. For personal injury protection, you may already be covered by your employer's health or disability insurance policy (call HR to ask about this), in which case just buy the required minimum.

Time Your Car Insurance Purchase, If You Can

Car insurance rates differ by when you purchase the plan. Car insurance rates tend to be cheapest in December by about 7.5 percent— which can add up big time over the years! and most expensive in March, according to InsuranceQuotes.com.

Ask About These Little-Known Insurance Discounts

Some of the most common car insurance discounts that you may already get include having a home policy with the same company, paying the bill upfront, and being married. But here are some discounts you've probably never heard of, because insurance companies often won't tell you unless you ask!

1. **Low mileage:** 13 percent of companies offer discounts of an average of 11 percent if you don't drive your car much (typically 7,000, 10,000, and 12,500 miles per year or less). *Average savings: $84 per year.*
2. **Advance renewal:** More than one in four insurance companies offer a deal for those who renew in advance (set a reminder on your Google calendar), typically seven to ten days ahead of schedule. The savings is 8 percent on average. *Average savings: $61 per year.*

3. **Customer loyalty:** More than one in three companies give discounts for consumers who have been customers for twelve months, thirty-six months, and/or sixty months, with an average savings of 6 percent. *Average savings: $46 per year.*

4. **Homeownership:** People who own their homes can save an average of 6 percent. About one in five insurance companies offer this. *Average savings: $46 per year.*

   Source: Insure.com, 2013.

Tackle Your Car Insurance in Under 3 hours to Save an Estimated $350 This Year

These three steps can definitely be worthwhile. You can break this up into thirty-minute sessions each day, and still be done in a week!

Step 1: Know how much car insurance you need.
It should only take you about a half hour to figure out how much car insurance you need. See page 84 for further guidance, or use the Insurance.com calculator online. *Estimated time: 30 minutes.*

Step 2: Get 3 new quotes on car insurance.
Start with the NerdWallet.com comparison tool (see page 83) to find the three companies that have the estimated lowest rates. Next, call each company to get their quotes (this will take about an hour and a half total). If you call one company each day to get a quote (roughly thirty minutes per call), you're done with this process in three days. *Estimated time: 1.5 hours.*

Step 3: Switch your car insurance company if necessary.
Make sure to ask about their discounts. *Estimated time: 30 minutes.*

Sample Schedule

Monday	Calculate how much auto insurance you need. Use the NerdWallet.com comparison tool to get quotes on that amount. Write down the three companies with the lowest quotes. *Estimated time: 30 minutes.*
Tuesday	Call the first company to get a quote on auto insurance. If the quote comes in higher than you pay now, tell them—and ask them how to save. Write down that quote. The agent will try to get you to commit right on the spot, but wait it out so you can get multiple quotes. *Estimated time: 30 minutes or less.*
Wednesday	Call the second company to get a quote on auto insurance. If the quote comes in higher than you pay now, tell them—and ask them how to save. Write down that quote. *Estimated time: 30 minutes or less.*
Thursday	Call the third company to get a quote on auto insurance. If the quote comes in higher than you pay now, tell them—and ask them how to save. Write down that quote. *Estimated time: 30 minutes or less.*
Friday	Vet the company with the lowest quote. While NerdWallet looks at how well the companies treat their customers, you also want to check on the company's financial health. Go on AMBest.com and enter the

(Continued)

company's name and your state at the
search bar at the top; that will tell you
if the company is in good financial
standing. If there are any red flags,
move to the next lowest bid. Once you
determine the company with the lowest
offer that is well ranked and meets all your
minimum requirements (see page 84), call
them back and get that lower cost policy.
Estimated time: 30 minutes.

One MAJOR Thing You Can Do to Slash Car Costs

As of 2015, the average annual cost to own and operate a car was
$8,698, according to AAA, which includes gas, maintenance, tires,
insurance, license and registration fees, taxes, depreciation, and the
finance charges that go with driving a typical sedan 15,000 miles
each year. Whew, that's a lot! So it's worth considering whether your
family could make do with one car. Could you drop your spouse
at work and pick him up, maybe with the occasional Uber ride in
between when needed? For most families, I know, this would be difficult, but it can mean thousands extra in your pocket so it's worth
considering. And don't forget that you may make money when you
sell the second car. The Kellys—that's the couple who majorly downsized their house on page 50—netted about $3,000 and used that to
help pay down their debts.

Chapter 7

Education

A Smarter Way to Pay for School and College

Sure, we'd all love our kids to roam the ivied grounds of Harvard or Yale—or at least graduate from a state school without keg-standing their way to academic probation—but that comes at a hefty price. If college continues to climb at current rates, moms could easily face a six-figure price tag for college. Plus, parents will pay for tons of other school-related items even before the kids hit college, including tutoring, school supplies, extracurricular activities, tests, and possibly even private school. All in all, you could face a bill of well over a half a million dollars for a single child's education expenses.

But don't panic yet! In this chapter I'm going to show you what kinds of educational expenses you can expect and simple ways to pay for them, and I'm going to thoroughly tackle probably the most stressful one of all to parents: the cost of college.

The True Cost of Educating Your Kids

School supplies, test prep, extracurriculars, tutoring…the list of extras you'll pay to further your kids' education is, well, insane! Here's what you can expect.

What Parents Can Expect to Spend Each Year on Education			
	School Supplies	Extracurricular Costs and Other Fees	College Test Prep	Total Annual Cost
Elementary	$196	$463	N/A	$659
Middle School	$328	$629	N/A	$957
High School	$374	$832	$292	$1,498

Source: Huntington Backpack Index 2016.

So what's included in this chart? When it comes to school supplies, all the standard stuff that you tend to buy annually from pens and pencils to index cards and calculators. But beware: Pricey extras like a laptop or tablet are not included here, so you will need to factor in that cost, too. The average cost for a laptop is now around $500, and $260 for a tablet, though of course these can go higher.

The college test prep total listed for high school includes the ACT/SAT test prep book, AP test prep book, ACT/SAT test fees, and AP test fees. If your child goes to an ACT/SAT class or gets tutoring, expect to spend more.

Extracurricular costs include things like music stands, gym uniforms, and fees for school, music rental, field trips, sports participation, and band. Here are average costs nationwide for different extracurriculars, according to American Express:

Sports	$195
Music	$152
Other hobby groups	$110
Volunteer activities	$138
Art programs	$148

Source: American Express.

Though this data is helpful, keep in mind that it's an average. Music can cost the most (sometimes $300 per year or more) thanks in large part to the fact that instruments are so pricey. Sports participation fees can also run into the hundreds of dollars. Should your child take up a sport outside of school that's pricey (hello, horseback riding!) you may have to tack on an extra zero to your annual extracurricular costs. Data provided by Care.com in 2016 shows that about one in three families spend $1,000 or more on a child's extracurricular activities in a year.

A Savvy Way to Save on Extracurriculars (That You're Actually Willing to Do)

Because extracurriculars often cost so much, here's my advice: Don't assume your child will stick to a sport or activity and purchase items accordingly. Because let's get real, how many sports and activities did *you* actually stick with? If your child wants to play a musical instrument, rent the equipment until you are sure he likes it—sites like Music & Arts (musicarts .com) and RentMyInstrument.com make that easy. For sports equipment, get it used—try sites like SwapMeSports.com and brick-and-mortar stores like Play It Again Sports. For pretty much anything, it's worth checking out eBay, Amazon, Freecycle, and Craigslist. Use mommy groups and Listservs to ask parents if anyone has the equipment and if you can purchase it on the cheap or swap for it. Ask moms of older kids if their children have outgrown any gear that they want to get rid of; and you may even want to post a message on Facebook. *Average savings: $100 or more per year.*

What Will I Pay for a Tutor?

If your child needs tutoring, the rates vary a lot depending on where you live—and tend to get more expensive as a child gets older. Data from Care.com shows that private tutors for high school students start at $10 to $15 per hour, but those with specialized experience can easily cost $75 an hour (yikes!). A tutor from an agency might start at about $25 per hour. The bottom line here: You can, and should, negotiate these prices.

Private School: It's Not Just for the Super Rich

Private schools cost an average of $7,770 per year for elementary school kids and more than $13,000 for older kids, according to 2011–12 data from the National Center for Education Statistics; in some big cities like New York and L.A. those costs can triple. Religious schools, like Catholic schools, tend to be a few thousand a year cheaper. Even so, you can't always write off private school because public school is "cheaper." In many cases, owning a home in an area with excellent public schools is very pricey. Sometimes the median home price in those areas is two times the national average or more. An analysis done by ATTOM Data Solutions found that housing is unaffordable for the average family in the vast majority of school districts with good public schools. Yikes!

So does private school make sense? Of course. There are also, as you know, plenty of reasons beyond the financial to consider it. But I'll leave those to you and just focus on helping you figure out if it makes financial sense. First, you must compare your housing costs, including property taxes (which can be very high in good school districts) in a good school district and a not-so-good school district. Use a site like Trulia, Zillow, or Realtor.com to get started; though their tax estimates aren't always entirely accurate they should give you a rough idea. Factor in commuting costs, if you have to go a far distance for work, as well. If the housing costs in a not-so-good school district plus the annual cost of private tuition are less than the costs of housing in a good school district, then private school can make financial sense.

How to Pay for Private School

It used to be that 529 plans were just for paying for college, but starting in 2018, you can pay for private school with a 529 plan. As of the writing of this book, you can pull $10,000 per year in tax-free withdrawals from your 529 savings for private elementary through high school. You can learn more about how 529 plans work on page 102.

Beyond the 529, there aren't a ton of options for fancy savings vehicles for precollege private school. So you're probably going to have to do the hard work of budgeting and saving for this cost each month. But it's important to remember a few things you can do to save. First, sometimes private school tuition is negotiable—and you won't know unless you ask about what discounts you can get. Some schools will give you a discount for:

* Paying tuition in cash
* Paying the entire year's tuition upfront
* If you refer other students to the school
* If you have more than one child at the school
* If you work (or volunteer) at the school

You should also ask about all scholarships and merit-based awards, as well as financial aid, which is usually based on a family's ability to pay. Plus, in more than a dozen states, you may be able to get a state-funded voucher to help pay for private school—look on the NCSL.org site for more details on this. Many private schools also have Scrip or TRIP programs that give you tuition rebates when you buy certain gift cards through the school.

A Savvy Way to Save on School Supplies (That You're Actually Willing to Do)

Once you've grabbed the basics like pens, pencils, and notebooks at Office Depot (look for their one-cent deals, which they offer occasionally when you spend $5 or more) and the almost-always-super-cheap dollar store—or the old standbys like Target, Walmart, Sam's, and Costco—consider this perhaps counterintuitive advice: Hit up Staples for brand-name items. Staples has a little-known 110 percent price match guarantee policy, which means that if you buy an item there and then see it for less elsewhere, including on Amazon, the store will match the lower price and give you a 10 percent discount on top of that. That policy is among the best in the retail business, though beware, the item at the lower price has to be identical to the one you bought in the store.

How to Plan and Save for Your Child's College Education

Yes, it's time to tackle one of the biggest financial hurdles parents face—paying for college. Before we get into how to do that, I want you to know that it is absolutely doable. Even a mom who went through a divorce and started her own company is able to pay for her kid's college. Just ask communications specialist Michelle Faulkner, who is on track to fully pay for her teenage daughter and son to go to college, as long as they choose an in-state school. She started saving in a 529 plan when her son was born, and put in just about $100 a month. "That was all we could afford," she explains. Just three years later, it was even tougher to save, as Michelle was going through a divorce, which meant that to save for her kids' college, she had to make big sacrifices. "I cut almost every nonessential—no eating out, bare bones cable, no new clothes for myself," she says. "I even tried coloring my own hair, which was a disaster!" But she kept at it, and slowly began ratcheting up her savings as her income grew.

For Michelle, who watched some of her own peers struggle with student debt, the sacrifices she's made are worth it. "I think this will make their twenties a lot less stressful," she says. "I can't believe the debt that some young adults are now shouldering for their education." She's right about that: The average student with loans now graduates with more than $30,000 in debt, and all that debt is impacting their lives. Fully 56 percent of millennials (compared to 43 percent of adults overall) with student loan debt say that this debt has prevented them from doing things they'd like, such as buying a home, getting married, having kids, or buying a car, according to data released by Bankrate.com in 2016.

No doubt, every parent wants to save for their kid's college, but

I know you may feel you can't. The good news: It doesn't take a ton of money to save a chunk of change. Even if you can't save the full amount, remember this: Saving something is better than saving nothing.

Saving for College with Just $10, $25, or $50 a Week

You can put away a lot less than six figures and still fund your child's education. Seriously, socking away just $10, $25, or $50 per week (and come on, I know you could find at least an extra $10 per week!) can yield you a lot more savings than you might expect. Save just $10 a week for the next fifteen years in one of the handy-dandy college savings plans and you could end up saving more than $11,500 to pay for college, assuming you get a 5 percent annual return on investment. (Don't worry if this sounds complicated, I'll walk you through it in this chapter.) Up that to $25 per week, and you're at nearly $30,000; and if you can swing to $50 a week, you're at nearly $58,000.

Saving for College with Just $10, $25, or $50 per Week

Total savings if you get a 5 percent average annual return on your investment.

	After 6 years	After 9 years	After 12 years	After 15 years	After 18 years
Save $10 per week					
You've put in	$3,120	$4,680	$6,240	$7,800	$9,360
You've saved	$3,626	$5,879	$8,486	$11,504	$14,999

	After 6 years	After 9 years	After 12 years	After 15 years	After 18 years
	Save $25 per week				
You've put in	$7,800	$11,700	$15,600	$19,500	$23,400
You've saved	$9,066	$14,697	$21,215	$28,761	$37,497
	Save $50 per week				
You've put in	$15,600	$23,400	$31,200	$39,000	$46,800
You've saved	$18,132	$29,394	$42,431	$57,522	$74,993

You may now be thinking: *But that's still not enough to fully pay for college.* And you're probably right. But guess what? THAT'S OKAY! Something saved is better than nothing saved. Because here's the thing: For every $1 that your child has to borrow for college, he'll probably end up paying about $2 to repay the loan. So every little bit you can contribute can save him a TON down the road.

Quick Tip

Don't Be Afraid to Ask for a College Donation for the Holidays

Grandma and Grandpa, no doubt, want to see the joy on your kids' faces when they open their physical gifts for the holidays. But it's okay to ask them to consider buying a less expensive physical gift for the kids and putting a little money—even if it's just $10—toward

Junior's college. While he may not love that on Christmas morning, I guarantee you he'll appreciate it more than a disposable toy down the road!

What Will College Cost in the Future?

You may be wondering: How much do I need to save to pay for my kid's college? Telling you the figures for a recent year is pretty easy: A student attending college in 2016–17 would face college costs (including tuition, fees, and room and board) of more than $20,000 per year for a public, four-year state school and more than $45,000 per year for a private four-year school. Spend the usual four years at these places and you'll have a bill of more than $80,000 and $180,000 respectively.

It gets a bit harder to predict those costs into the future, but it's worth doing because how else will you know how much to save? If we assume college costs will rise 3 percent a year (and let me just tell you, this is conservative, so you will likely face an even bigger bill than this chart is showing you!), here are the costs your child might face down the road. You can also play with these numbers using Vanguard's College Savings Planner, which you can find on the Vanguard website or on my website.

Sticker Price Shocker		
The Estimated Price Tag for 4 Years of College Down the Road		
If your child will start attending college in . . .	Public, in-state school	Private, nonprofit school
2019	$91,000+	$207,000+
2022	$100,300+	$226,000+

If your child will start attending college in...	Public, in-state school	Private, nonprofit school
2025	$109,000+	$247,000+
2028	$119,000+	$270,000+
2031	$130,000+	$295,000+
2034	$143,000+	$323,000+

Source: These are rough estimates based on 2016–17 tuition, fees, and room and board costs in 2016-17 from CollegeBoard.org; assumes a 3 percent annual rate of inflation.

What You'll Really Pay for College Out of Pocket

Okay, good, you haven't slammed this book closed in sheer terror at those numbers. (Or, if you did, you've opened it again!) You'll be glad to know there *is* good news—you may only have to pay about half of this cost out of your own pocket! Most families do not pay the sticker price for college thanks to scholarships, grants, and financial aid that offset the cost. You can play around with College Scorecard at CollegeScorecard.ed.gov, the government's site that lists the average annual cost that people actually pay for certain schools, to get an idea of this. According to College Board data from the 2015–16 year, the average family only pays about 42 percent of the sticker price listed for tuition and fees at many four-year schools. However, it's important to note that higher income families may assume more of the cost than lower-income families, so take that into account.

Momsanity Tip: Dealing with the Dreaded FAFSA Form

You've probably heard about the FAFSA—which stands for Free Application for Federal Student Aid—and you'll probably be filling one out soon enough, as this is the form that lets you apply for grants, loans, scholarships, and work-study money for your college-going child. In other words, this is how to get your child money for going to college, yay! I'm not going to inundate you with all the details here, except to tell you what I think is one of the best resources out there for figuring this all out: StudentAid.ed.gov. It will walk you through whether you might be eligible for aid and how to fill out the FAFSA and apply for it.

A Smart Alternative to Four Years of Tuition

For many families I know, even saving for half of the sticker price for college might not be an option. Here's something to consider if that's the case: Have your child attend community college for a year or two, which is typically a fraction of the cost, and then transfer into her dream school to finish her degree. That can significantly reduce college costs and she still gets a degree from a résumé-enhancing school. And think about it: On a résumé, you generally only put your school name, GPA, and graduation year.

How to Shop Smart by Getting Cash Back for College

If you're going to be buying stuff anyway, it may make sense to get cash back on this spending that goes directly into a college savings plan for the kiddies. Are these offers always going to give you the most cash back? No. But if you're a mom who doesn't want to think about saving for college (or dealing with different cash-back sites/ cards and then moving that cash into a 529 plan), these may be good options.

1. Upromise.com

You shop, they give you cash back that goes into a 529 plan or a goals savings account for your kids. There are two main ways to use their service.

First, you can log in to your Upromise.com account, shop at one of the 850+ participating retailers, and get cash back, which is usually 5 percent or more. They also have partnerships with certain restaurants, gas stations, and travel sites, so you can get cash back from those, too. (Warning: Do not let this spur you into unnecessary shopping!)

The second is to get their MasterCard. *Only do this if you are 100 percent certain you can pay off your bill in full each month.* It gives you 1 percent cash back on all purchases. You also get 5 percent back at certain restaurants, online shopping sites, and travel sites. Yes, you can get better cash back elsewhere. NerdWallet.com is a great resource for finding the best cash-back and other cards. But if you know you're the kind of person who won't then put that cash back toward college savings—and you really want to save toward college—this isn't a bad bet.

2. Rewards Credit Cards

Here are a few other college savings cards to consider:

○ **Fidelity Investment Rewards Visa Card**—gives 2 percent cash back (a very good rate) that can go into a Fidelity-managed 529 plan. Check to see if your state has this

option—as of the writing of this book, it was just available in Delaware, Massachusetts, New Hampshire, and
Arizona.

○ **Alabama CollegeCounts Rewards Visa Card**—will deposit
your rewards into your Alabama 529 plan. You can find
details at CollegeCounts529.com.

○ **Illinois Bright Directions 529 Rewards Visa Card**—will
deposit your rewards into your Illinois 529 plan. You can
find details at BrightDirections.com.

To use these and all rewards credit cards in a financially savvy
way, you must pay the balance off in full and on time each month.
That's because the interest you'll pay if you don't pay your balance
in full is typically far more than you earn in rewards. Plus, you
must familiarize yourself with the cash-back rewards structure. The
UPromise Mastercard has a particularly annoying (though sometimes lucrative) rewards structure, so you just need to make sure
you understand what you get 1 percent versus 2 to 5 percent cash
back on.

What You Need to Know about 529 Plans

A 529 plan is simply an education savings plan operated by a state
or an educational institution. Typically, the money you invest in your
state's plan can be used to pay for college even if your child goes
to school in a different state than you live in. The big advantage
of these is that the federal government will not tax your earnings
from the plan when you take the money out to pay for school; there
are tax advantages on the state level in most states, too. The state tax
benefits are why it often—but not always—pays to invest in your own
state's 529 plan. You can, however, invest in another state's plan;

U.S. *News & World Report* offers a simple article on why you might want to do this entitled "4 Reasons to Consider Purchasing Another State's 529 Plan."

THE ONE THING

If You Only Do One Thing to Save for Your Kids' College, Do This

Open a 529 plan and contribute to it.

For most people, this is the smartest way to save for your kids' college, as it can lead to thousands (yes, thousands!) of extra dollars saved for your kid's education versus other savings options. You contribute to the account, the money is invested, and you can pull out the money you earn, tax-free, to pay for tuition and other college-related expenses for your kids.

There are generally two types:

1. **Prepaid Tuition Plan**—You pay for a year of tuition, typically at an in-state public school, in advance at a locked-in price. No matter how much tuition goes up, you will be paying it at your locked-in price.
2. **Traditional 529 Plan**—You invest the money how you see fit and use that money to pay for college expenses at a wide variety of colleges.

Most experts prefer the traditional 529 plans over the prepaid tuition plans thanks, in part, to the fact that the traditional plans tend to have more flexibility. I'll spare you the details here, but if you're curious about why, Savingforcollege.com breaks that all out. So if you just want to open a plan and move on (I hear you, sometimes it's better just to get something done rather than stalling in panic), pick your state's traditional 529 plan (not the prepaid tuition plan) and move on.

The money you earn in these plans must be used for school expenses (you face a 10 percent penalty if you withdraw it to pay for something else), though you can transfer it from family member to family member, so you can use the money for any of your children.

Opening a 529 Plan for Your Kids in Just Three Steps

Many parents get freaked out by the idea of opening a 529 plan because they have to do things like pick investments. I'm going to help you, so don't you let this be a barrier for you! I'm going to give you a few simple rules right now just to get you over that hump. These aren't permanent, they are just choices to make to get you through the huge step of opening a 529 plan. (We'll look at more details on investing the easy way later in the book.) For now, just remember, this is your kid's future and you have to start somewhere; so start here!

Opening a 529 plan shouldn't take you more than about an hour TOTAL. I've broken this hour into three steps that you can do during a given week (maybe Monday, Tuesday, and Wednesday night after the kids go to bed).

Step 1: Make Sure Your State's Plan Is Up to Snuff

Each year, financial firm Morningstar ranks 529 plans. Almost all of them rank at least neutral (and even a neutral plan is likely still appealing to many in-state residents because of the tax breaks 529 plans offer). In 2016, just three ranked negative, which means you may want to avoid those three. Make sure your state's plan ranks neutral or above. You can find Morningstar's rankings on their website at www.morningstar.com or on my website. *Estimated time: 15 minutes.*

Step 2: Gather the Necessary Information

To open a 529 plan, you generally need your and your child's names, birthdates, addresses, and social security numbers; and bank account information, like account number and routing number so you can make a deposit on the spot and set up automatic contributions. Often if you set up automatic deposits, they will let you make an initial deposit of as little as $50. Without automatic contributions each month, the initial deposit is usually much higher. *Estimated time: 15 minutes.*

Step 3: Enroll in the 529 Plan

Go to Savingsforcollege.com, click the big map right on their home page, find your state, and simply click "enroll now" under Consumer Plans and you can open an account. Seriously, this is a few clicks and bam, you're ready to open one! You can also google your state's 529 plan and follow the instructions right on the plan's site.

If you have two or more options, as some states do, remember, in most cases, you do NOT want the prepaid tuition plan, and you want the plan that Morningstar ranks higher. Savingforcollege.com also has plan rankings right on the site, so together the sites make this super easy to pick a plan. Enter in all the information I had you gather above, putting your child as the beneficiary of the account. *Estimated time: 30 minutes.*

How to Start Using Your 529 Plan

Now that your account is set up, the hardest part is the investment choices, which are typically a range of different mutual funds. A mutual fund is simply a collection of different stocks, bonds, or other investments. Each plan has different investment options; if you've ever chosen your 401(k) investments you'll have an idea of what this will be like. I'll walk you through picking investments on pages 221–222, so skip ahead to that section if you have an extra 30 minutes or so to dig into this now. If that seems too daunting or annoying, I'll show you how to find a financial planner to help you on page 219.

You can change your investment choices twice a year. So if you want to open the account and just pick something for now to save for Junior's college, that's fine. Even if you don't pick the perfect investment, it at least helps you clear that psychological hurdle (yay, mama!) of starting to save for college. Often these plans have investments tailored to the age of your child. That investment option will usually be clearly labeled so you know what ages it's suitable for, so those are a decent right-now choice for parents.

If all of this sounds like a lot of work, I can tell you—it's really not. I recently opened a 529 plan for my daughter in New York and I swear to you, it took me less than 30 minutes.

Other College Savings Options

While most experts say the 529 plan is many parents' best bet, there are other options. Some parents use their Roth IRAs to save for college. This works as long as you're going to be fifty-nine-and-a-half when your child is in college. If you'll be younger than that, you'll pay penalties for withdrawing the money early. Savings-forcollege.com is a great resource for you to learn about all of your options.

Your Retirement Savings vs. the College Fund

Look, for most parents, it's simply not realistic to save up the entirety of college costs for their kids. For one, you MUST put your own retirement savings first. Your kids can get a loan for college, but you can't get one for retirement. If you're not already socking away 12 percent or more of your income into your 401(k) or other retirement savings plan, don't start dumping money into a 529 plan. Even if you are on track with your retirement savings, the reality is that adding major college savings on top of this may not be feasible. The bottom line: Save as much as you can, but don't freak out. Kids can get financial aid for college, they can get scholarships, they can get grants, they can do a work-study program. Sure, in an ideal world, you'd pay for the entirety of their college out of your pocket, but most of us don't live in an ideal world. Can you aim to save for a third of their college costs? What about half? Don't fall into the trap of black-and-white thinking: *If I can't save for it all, why bother.* Just do what you can. Anything you can save for them is money they won't have to pay back down the road.

7 Simple Ways to Earn Big Bucks Without Having to Work Too Hard for It

I know you don't have a million extra hours to find a second job. You already know to do things like host a garage sale, put your stuff up on eBay and Craigslist, and get cash back using a site like Ebates .com. But there are some other easy ways to earn a chunk of change (I'm not even bothering with things that pay only a few bucks here) without having to put forth too much effort. Here are several:

1. **Going on vacation? Put your house on Airbnb or VRBO.** Depending on where you live and how large your home is, this could yield $100 or more a night. I have a friend who pays for nearly all of his vacations this way!

2. **Put your services on TaskRabbit.com.** Yes, this is technically "another job" but you are free to take the gigs you want that work within your schedule and set your own price, which can top $20 an hour in some areas. You can do anything from run errands to pack boxes to clean for others. It may also be worth considering becoming a virtual assistant (you can sometimes do this on your own hours) using sites like VirtualAssistants.com.

3. **Pet sit or walk a dog with DogVacay.com.** It's typically a pretty easy way to earn $10 to $30 or so a night. Way easier than babysitting kids, let me tell you! Just make sure the dog is good around kids!

4. **Become part of a focus group at FocusGroup.com.** Some pay $75 to $150! These could take one to two hours or more; sometimes you can do these kinds of things from home, other times you might have to go into an office or event space.

5. **Switch banks.** Sometimes you can get $50 to $200 when you open a new checking or savings account. Each month, Nerd Wallet.com lists banks with great signing bonuses. Just be sure you can meet any requirements the bank has (minimum balance, et cetera) and that the account is a free checking or savings account (i.e., no monthly fee).

6. **Get paid to take a commute you're doing anyway with Roadie.com.** This service connects people who need something delivered—ranging from legal papers to a dog collar to a pet—with someone driving that way anyway. Depending on length of drive and what it is, you can sometimes earn $100 or more; it's free to join.

7. **Sell your electronics on Gazelle.com or NextWorth.com.**
No doubt, you have old cell phones, Xboxes, and other electronics that your kids have deemed "so over." Sell them on these sites to earn cash (sometimes $100 or more depending on the device!).

Momsanity Advice

Q: How do I deal with "mom guilt" of not being able to afford a top-notch education for the kids?

A: Writer Alina Adams, her husband, and their three kids live in a two-bedroom apartment, and they've been frugal their entire lives—no video games or trendy clothes for the kids, no tutors for the SATs and other tests. Adams says she's doesn't feel a lick of guilt about not being able to buy the kids those extras. But there is one thing she feels mom guilt about: not being able to afford to send her son to the college of his choice. "As a result, he is applying to twenty-one schools this fall: Not because he isn't a good candidate who fears he won't get in anywhere (he's already in at a few places), but because he is applying to schools that offer merit aid, hoping to hit on one we'll be able to afford," she explains. "He worked so hard for this, and I'd like to be able to tell him he can go to any school that accepts him, but that's just not an option for us, and that makes me feel guilty."

I interviewed dozens of moms for this book, and most of them expressed one version or another of this guilt. While many didn't often lose sleep over not being able to afford the material things they wanted for their kids, when it came to not being able to afford college or other educational things like the "right" private school or tutoring, they began to freak out. Mom, take heart: For one, your kids can get loans to go to school and they can work part-time while attending if they need cash; just because you didn't save doesn't mean they can't go to college at all. But perhaps most importantly: Research shows that some of the greatest predictors of success in life are things like determination, grit, and hours and hours of practice—things that you can easily teach your children yourself (and for free) and that don't require a diploma from a fancy school. What's more, you don't want your kids thinking that to get your love and approval they need to succeed. "They need to know that they can't judge their worth based on an outcome," says psychologist Elizabeth Lombardo.

Chapter 8

Health Care
*The (Financially) Healthy
Way to Get and Stay Well*

Between making your health care plan options more confus-
ing than a college-level calculus course (ensuring that the
customer service rep has absolutely no health care experience and
answers you in script-speak) and denying claims they should be
paying, health insurance companies get an A+ when it comes to
inspiring a good, old-fashioned mommy tantrum. Seriously, your
two-year-old has got nothing on what you'll unleash on your insurance company should they try to mess with you and your sick kid!
This chapter will help you figure out how to navigate the nightmare
that is your health insurance plan—and how, when, and why to
switch plans if needed.

But first I just want to remind you that health insurance is
ALWAYS necessary. Don't go a day without it. Need some proof?
Medical bills are the number one cause of bankruptcies in America,
according to a study by financial website NerdWallet. Additionally,
more than half of people without health insurance say they have
struggled to afford a medical bill in the past year, just 20 percent
with insurance say the same, according to a poll by the *New York*

Times and the Kaiser Family Foundation. And among those 20 percent, it's likely for some that if they had a better health plan, they wouldn't be in the situation they're in now.

But the biggest reasons you MUST have good health insurance: You need to be able to a) protect your kids' health at all times, and b) protect your own health so you can be strong for them for their entire lives. Few things are as basic and important as good health. And that's why this chapter is essential reading.

Picking the Right Health Insurance Plan

One of the most important things you can do to save money on health care is to pick the right plan. And that's no easy task. I'm going to assume you have a health plan already, but come November (or whenever you or your spouse's open enrollment is) you're going to want to review your coverage to make sure you have the right plan for your family. This is a snore, but worth it for the peace of mind you'll have.

Six Health Insurance Terms to Know

1. **Deductible:** Often you must spend a certain amount of money—anywhere from a couple hundred to thousands of dollars depending on your plan—in a given year before your insurance company will begin picking up the tab. Note that some things like preventative services (annual wellness exams, pap smears, some shots, et cetera) are free to you—no deductible or out-of-pocket costs at all.

2. **Copay:** A fixed amount you must pay for a service like a visit to the doctor or a prescription; often it's between about $10 and $50 for a doctor's visit.

3. **Flexible spending account:** A savings account that you can put pretax dollars into for copays and other medical expenses. Those with PPO, POS, and HMO plans can use this, but not those with HDHP (I'll give you the details on these plans on page 114). Using a flexible spending account (FSA) can save you a ton of money on health care—see page 118 for an example of how valuable this is—but you don't want to put too much money in it because if you don't use all the money, you may lose it at the end of the year—though some people are able to carry over up to $500 into the following year.

4. **Coinsurance:** The percentage of the cost of a medical bill that you must pay out of your pocket. So, assuming you'd already met your deductible, if you had a $100 bill from the doctor's office and your coinsurance was 20 percent, you'd pay $20 of the bill and your insurance company would pay the rest.

5. **Out-of-pocket maximum:** The amount you must spend out of your own pocket (excluding the cost of your premiums) before your insurance company begins picking up 100 percent of the tab.

6. **Premium:** What you pay for your insurance. If you get it through your employer, they usually automatically deduct the cost from your paycheck.

Let me show you an example so you can understand how this all works together. Let's say you have a deductible of $1,000, your coinsurance is 20 percent and your out-of-pocket maximum is $5,000—and you get a serious illness. You'll pay *all* the medical costs for your treatment until you hit $1,000 (your deductible). After that, you'll pay 20 percent of the treatment costs and your insurance company will pay 80 percent (because that's your coinsurance rate). When your out-of-pocket costs for the year hit $5,000 (this includes your deductible), the insurance company pays the entire bill for the rest of the year.

The Four Types of Employer-Offered Health Insurance

Here are the types of plans your job may offer you—and how to pick the one that's right for you:

❋ **HMO (health maintenance organization):** This plan will only cover the costs of you seeing a doctor in the plan's network of doctors, so check the network ahead of time to see if your doctors are in it. It usually requires you to pick a primary care doctor. The good news with this plan is that it's one of the cheapest options—premiums are usually lower than a PPO plan, and there is typically no deductible or a very low one. The bad news is that the network of doctors isn't always the best and you usually need a referral to see a specialist or get certain tests done, which is annoying and delays you getting the care you need.

❋ Get this plan if you like the network of doctors, need to save money, and have the time and patience to deal with seeing your primary care doctor when you might need a specialist. Note that an EPO plan is like an HMO plan but has a national network of doctors instead of just a regional one.

Pros: Low cost

Cons: Less flexibility in choice of doctors, more time consuming to deal with

❋ **PPO (preferred provider organization):** This plan offers a lot more flexibility than an HMO. You can see a doctor who's not in the plan's network and the plan will pay for some of that cost (typically about 70 percent) and you don't need a referral from a primary care physician to see a specialist. If you see a doctor in the plan's network, the PPO plan works a lot like the HMO plan (with a small copay and good coverage).

* Pick this plan if you want to be able to choose from a big selection of doctors and you can afford the premiums and deductible.

Pros: Most flexibility in choice of doctors
Cons: High cost

* **POS (point of service):** This is basically a hybrid HMO and PPO plan. While, like with an HMO, you have a primary care doctor who must give you referrals to see specialists, it also (like a PPO) will cover some of the costs of seeing an out-of-network doctor (just not as much as a PPO plan would cover). This plan tends to be cheaper than a PPO, but more expensive than an HMO. This is a nice middle ground for someone who wants a PPO plan because of its flexibility in covering doctors who might not be in-network but can't afford the PPO plan.

Pros: Flexibility in choice of doctors; lower cost than PPO
Cons: Higher cost than an HMO; covers less of the cost of out-of-network doctors than a PPO plan

* **High-deductible health plan:** These plans have the lowest annual premiums, but, as you may have guessed, have a high deductible. Typically you'll have to pay about $2,500 out of pocket before the plan begins covering any medical expenses; but once you hit that number, it usually covers 100 percent. The plan is good for someone who doesn't need to see a doctor regularly and is on a serious budget. This plan is typically combined with an HSA (health savings account), an account that lets you save pretax dollars for health expenses, or an HRA, a health savings account funded by your employer.

Pros: Lowest premiums of all plans
Cons: May face high costs if you need to see a doctor

Quick Tip

Health Savings Account (HSA)

If you're offered an HSA, it can be super lucrative to use it. Depending on your tax bracket, you could easily save $1,000 or more in taxes for every $5,000 you contribute to it.

How Much Does Health Insurance Really Cost?

Even when your employer helps out with the cost of your health insurance, it isn't cheap. And that's truer now than ever. Of course, your costs will vary dependently on your employer and family. But if you're wondering how your costs compare, this chart will show you what the average individual with an employer health insurance plan will pay each year to insure her family. (This is just what the individual pays; the employer then pays their part on top of this.)

Average Annual Health Insurance Premiums for a Family	
HMO	$5,389
PPO	$5,569
HDHP with savings option	$4,289

Source: Kaiser/HRET Survey of Employer-Sponsored Health Benefits, 2016.

If all this makes your head spin, I get it. Many moms I know opt for the PPO plan because for them, spending the extra money has been worth it because it gives peace of mind that their family can see any doctor they want and it will be covered to some degree, and it's less annoying (seriously, getting referrals is a huge hassle some-times!) than the other plans. But the important thing is that you get the best plan you can afford. Period.

Non-Employer-Based Health Insurance

If you don't get health insurance through your or your spouse's job—or if you plan on working for yourself in the future (go mama!)—you're going to need to buy health insurance. You can do this on one of the health care exchanges created by the Affordable Care Act (ACA)—aka Obamacare—or you can buy it through an individual health insurance company.

If you're not making bank, you will probably want to buy the plan through the health care exchanges, because lower-income people qualify for subsidies to help offset the cost of their health care when they shop this way. You can shop for a plan on HealthCare.gov or on your state's health care website. If you don't know if you're eligible for a subsidy, use the simple calculator from the Kaiser Family Foundation on their website (kff.org), which can tell you if you're eligible for a subsidy.

You can still buy your insurance on the exchanges even if you don't qualify for the subsidies, but you can also find a plan online. PolicyGenius.com will compare ACA plans and off-exchange plans, and you can also try sites like eHealthInsurance.com or Insure.com. If you're going to get a plan through the exchanges, they break out the plans—Platinum, Gold, Bronze, and Silver—and who they make sense for in a pretty straightforward way. I know, the sites got a bad rap, but their explanation of the different plans is actually decent! Go to HealthCare.gov and get started.

Saving Time with Insurance Brokers

If you don't want to deal with comparing plans yourself, you can use an independent insurance broker. You can find a list of them at NAHU.org. They are free for you to use and make their money from commissions paid to them by insurance companies.

Call a few brokers before you pick one. Here are three things to look for:

1. Make sure the agent you choose represents a number of companies and not just one company, because then he's only going to offer you plans from that company and they may be more expensive.
2. Ask about things like professional memberships he or she belongs to (like the National Association of Insurance and Financial Advisors or the Independent Insurance Agents and Brokers of America).
3. Listen to what they ask you. They should be asking nuanced questions about your health needs to find you a good policy.

THE ONE THING

If You Do One Thing to Save on Health Care this Year, Do This

Once you've got a good health insurance plan, likely the biggest thing you can do to save on health care is this: Use your flexible spending account (FSA). FSA allows you to put in up to $2,600 (as of 2017) of pretax money to save for many health-related costs. This can yield you big savings: If you maxed out your FSA and were in the 30 percent tax bracket that might yield about $800 in savings on health care costs for the year!

So how do you use your FSA? It's easy:

Step 1: Determine What Your Health-Related Spending Will Be This Year

Look back at last year: Estimate how much you spent on doctor and dental visits, copays, prescriptions, contacts and glasses, and other health care services. I scan my bank accounts online from the past year to get the number. What do you think it will be (conservatively) this year? That's how much you'll want to contribute to your FSA. Remember, be conservative about this because any money you don't use in this account within the year, you may lose. Check with your HR department for more details, some plans roll some of the funds over to the next year, while others don't. *Estimated time: 30 minutes.*

Step 2: Sign Up for your FSA During Open Enrollment

This will take you no time at all! You simply elect how much you want to put in your FSA and poof, you're done! *Estimated time: 30 minutes.*

FSA Use It or Lose It Tips

If there's money left and the year is closing in on you fast, here are some ways to spend your FSA dollars:

1. Get your doctor to write you a prescription for over-the-counter drugs that you might use in the coming year (pain relievers, allergy medications, cough-and-cold medicines, et cetera) and buy them.
2. Order a six-month supply of contact lenses and solution.

3. Stock up on sunscreen, bandages, and any other items you need with the FSA symbol on the price tag at the store.

A quick Google search will show you a full list of what an FSA will cover.

The 3 Things You Must Know Before You Pick a Health Plan

Of course, you should read all the fine print on your insurance plan before you pick it, but let's get real here: Who has time to do that? So let me make this simple for you: Just remember these three things that will help you pick the best plan. All of this information can typically be found on your insurance company's website. But if you have any questions on these, call your human resources department or the insurance company and ask them to walk you through all of this.

1. **The coverage:** What procedures and other things are covered—and which aren't? Get the Summary of Benefits for the plan on your insurer's website to find out. Generally, plans cover: emergency services, lab tests, hospitalization, maternity and newborn care, substance abuse treatment, mental health treatment, outpatient care, pediatric services including dental and vision, prescription drugs, preventive care, and rehabilitation service.

2. **The cost:** What's your monthly out-of-pocket cost for the plan? What are your copays, coinsurance, and deductible? What is the out-of-pocket maximum?

3. **The network:** What's the network of doctors and hospitals like? Are your doctors in the network or out of network? How much more will you pay if a doctor is out of network?

Momsanity Tip: Find Out the Costs BEFORE They Come in the Mail

I know you probably aren't going to read the fine print on your health plan, and I totally get that. Here's what I do: If a doctor says I may need a certain medication or treatment, and I don't know how much will be covered or the kind of bill I might expect when it's over, I simply call the insurance company and ask. The call usually doesn't take more than 20 minutes or so, and it prevents major surprises coming to me in the mail. If something isn't going to be fully covered, I know about it ahead of time and can do some extra saving, if needed.

It's also important to ask the names of all the medical providers who will be doing your treatment ahead of time. Sometimes one might be covered and another not, so you want to get this cleared up ahead of time. And, of course, check your bill for mistakes when it comes—they tend to be littered with mistakes that can easily add 20 percent or more to your tab. Call and ask about anything you're unsure of.

How to Save Thousands on the Cost of Pregnancy and Childbirth

Even with insurance, you may pay a lot for having a child; the average out-of-pocket cost is about $3,400 for someone with insurance. Of course, it may be far less (or far more)—but you have at least some degree of control over this.

Here are four things you can do to save yourself thousands:

1. Use the Network

One of the costliest things you can do during pregnancy and childbirth is to use an out-of-network doctor or opt for a nonessential service that the insurance company won't cover. That's why as soon as you get pregnant, you should call your insurance company and get a list of everything it covers and doesn't cover for moms— doctors, specialists, hospitals, classes, birthing centers, drugs (you name it!) in the network. Here's a list things to ask your insurance company when you call them.

- What prenatal care, labor, and delivery services are covered by insurance?
- Are there services that aren't covered that I should be aware of?
- What ob-gyns and hospitals are covered by insurance? (If you're interested in a birthing center or midwife, ask about coverage of those, too.)
- Do I need a referral to see an ob-gyn or other specialist?
- What maternity services require me to get preauthorization from the insurance company before I use them?
- What prenatal services (like genetic tests, ultrasounds, et cetera) are covered?
- How long of a hospital stay will you cover—and do you cover private rooms?

And remember, throughout your pregnancy and childbirth, don't be afraid to call them and ask "Is this covered?" if you aren't sure. It's annoying but literally can save you hundreds, sometimes thousands in medical bills, so totally worth it. (Or milk the fact that you're carrying a human inside of you and make your spouse or a family member do it for you!)

2. Make the Most of Open Enrollment

Switch plans if necessary, picking one that will pick up more of the costs. Now may be the time to opt for that PPO, even though it may be pricier at the offset, as it will reimburse you for out-of-network doctors to some degree (while an HMO won't). Think about it: You may want a certain specialist—this is your baby's life after all—but this wouldn't be covered under an HMO. Or during childbirth, an out-of-network doctor or anesthesiologist or other professional could step in, and you will likely be in no position to argue about that. Under a PPO plan, you at least would get some of that covered.

3. Max Out Your FSA

As noted above, the money you set aside in your FSA for out-of-pocket health expenses is tax-free. You're likely to use the maximum amount for the year, but double-check the amount you're setting aside against what you learn from your health insurance company about coverage. Just don't forget to include all your other nonpregnancy expenses.

4. Negotiate for Lower Prices and Ask for a Cash Discount

Go through the bills when they come (and boy will they come, one after the other, for months after your birth) and appeal any mistakes or charges that seem wrong. (See page 121.)

Momsanity Tip: Avoid Drowning in Bills

If you have a ton of claims denials and medical bills that are piling up, it may pay to hire a professional billing and claims specialist.

They're not cheap, but they can save you money in the long run if you're facing major bills. You can find them at BillAdvocates.com and Claims.org.

Can You Afford Maternity Leave?

If you're lucky, your employer gives you paid maternity leave. Most of us aren't so lucky—and federal law only requires that most employers (typically those with fifty or more employees) give women, who have worked at the company for at least a year, twelve weeks of unpaid leave when they give birth or adopt a child. Yes, UNPAID and even that is just twelve weeks. So not cool. A handful of states, including New Jersey, California, and Rhode Island, do supplement this with some paid leave.

Most of us will have to use some combination of sick days, personal days, vacation days, and short-term disability insurance to get the time off we need after birth. Many companies offer short-term disability insurance as part of your benefits package; it typically covers 40 to 60 percent of your salary for six weeks for a vaginal delivery and eight weeks for a C-section. Having to use vacation days for this is SUCH CRAP; never do you need vacation more than when you're a working mom and yet you had to burn it all to have a baby.

Here's how to handle this. First, talk to HR or your manager to figure out their maternity leave policy. Will the company give you any time off? Discuss your short-term disability policy if you have one (you can also get your insurance company to walk you through this). Ask what percentage of your salary the short-term disability policy will cover and whether there is a waiting period (called an elimination period; typically up to two weeks) before you can begin getting benefits. Next look at your paid vacation, personal, and sick days and see how many you can/are willing to cobble together. Once you know all of this, you can predict how long you can afford to be on maternity leave with your current savings.

If you started laughing when you read "current savings," you're not alone—many people don't have enough savings to cover taking off work. The good news: You may still be able to make this happen. Obviously, you should start making cuts in your spending (see Chapters 2–10) and pour that extra money into savings; plus you should try to earn a bit more. Personally, I think being pregnant is one of the best times to get rid of your stuff (gotta make room for the baby), so host a garage sale and earn some cash. Every little bit helps. Also see page 107 for ways to earn a little extra money without a lot of extra effort.

Sell It: 8 Little-Known Secrets for Making a Pile of Loot at a Garage Sale

1. **Time it right.** Saturday is the best day—and pick one when it should be warm out. It's also worth thinking about scheduling it right after people tend to get paid (right after the first of the month is usually a decent bet). Start early in the morning.

2. **Advertise a ton.** Tack up flyers at local coffee shops, churches, and other popular spots, and advertise online on sites like YardSaleSearch.com and Craigslist. Offer people who share a photo of your ad to their followers on Facebook or Twitter a 5 to 10 percent discount; this will help get the word out further. Ads should mention some of the awesome items you will be selling. And make sure on the day of the sale that your house is clearly marked with a big sign or balloons so people know they are at the right spot.

3. **Make it a group effort.** Bigger sales usually attract more buyers, so invite friends and neighbors to sell their stuff (as long as they post about the sale on their social networks and help you advertise). Make the sale seem lively and bustling so potential buyers will think this is the "hot" place to be.

4. **Offer a freebie.** It will cost you almost nothing to make a few pots of coffee, and buyers love a freebie. Put that freebie on your ad. Bonus: Research shows that once you've given someone a freebie they are more inclined to buy something from you.

5. **Offer bags to shoppers.** Ask friends and neighbors to give you their extra grocery bags; offer these to shoppers as they enter the sale. The reason: Research shows that giving people a bag or a cart when they shop encourages them to spend more—especially if you have a lot of small knickknacks to get rid of.

6. **Price it right.** As a very broad rule of thumb, price most items at about 75 percent off the original price you paid (exceptions include antiques and collectibles) and be prepared to lower those prices as people haggle. To determine more finely tuned pricing, look how much things are selling for on sites like Craigslist or eBay; it's not a bad idea to print out those listings so people can see they are getting a comparable (or even slightly better) price from you. Another tip: Make sure you have tons of change with you on the day of: Most people will bring twenties but will buy small things that are just a few bucks.

7. **Know what you'll sell—and what you won't.** In general, if you haven't used it in a couple years, you probably won't miss it if you sell it. A garage sale is a great place for selling things like this, including mass-produced, factory-made items like tools, clothes, books, household goods, and sports

equipment. Don't sell rare items or antiques here; they're usually best sold on collector's sites or a spot like eBay.

For the things you decide to sell online, consult one of the myriad online guides on how to do this best. Photos matter a lot (think well lit, from many angles, and make sure the items seems clean and in good condition), as does pricing and a detailed item description.

8. **Donate what's left—and get a tax break for it.** Take it to your local Goodwill or Salvation Army and keep a list of what you donated so you can possibly get a deduction at tax time. Goodwill has a suggested valuation guide on their site to figure out how much of a deduction you should take.

Simple Ways to Save on Health Care (That You're Actually Willing to Do)

Saving money on health care doesn't have to compromise the quality of the care. The single most expensive health care mistake is one you probably already know to avoid: going to an out-of-network doctor. Before you get a procedure done, make sure every doctor who will work on you is covered by your insurance. You should also ask your doctor or pharmacist if there are less expensive options that are equally as good and appeal charges on your bill that aren't legit. Some experts say up to half of all medical bills have errors on them. Beyond that, here are ten ways to save that many moms either don't know about or don't do.

1. **Be price-savvy about prescriptions.** Drugs can cost ten times more from one store to another, a *Consumer Reports* survey showed. You may never have thought about this because you simply fork over the copay for your drugs, but that, too,

may be a mistake. At some big-box stores and chains, prescriptions can be as little as $4 or so for a month's supply or $10 for a three-month stash. To shop around for prices, try GoodRx .com—you can also use the prices quoted there as a way to negotiate with your local pharmacy if they charge you more. Don't feel like comparison shopping? HealthWarehouse.com and Costco often have the lowest prices, a *Consumer Reports* study revealed.

2. **Ask about cash discounts.** Some hospitals, doctors, and other health care providers offer discounts—big ones—for those who pay cash up front. That's because so many people default or are late on their medical bills, so they're delighted to get payment up front.

3. **Negotiate.** One study found that two in three people who negotiated lower rates with their hospital or dentist got them, and three in five who negotiated with their doctor also succeeded. It helps to know what's a good price, and with health care that's difficult. There's no perfect way to do this, but start by checking websites like HealthcareBluebook.com.

4. **Shop smart.** Buy things like crutches and braces outside of the hospital. Pretty much every mom I know has had to deal with a sprain or broken bone with one of her kids. But beware, when you take them to the ER to deal with it, the crutches and braces they give them there will often have a significant markup. Buy them outside of the hospital to save.

5. **Dental discounts.** For routine cleanings and other simple procedures, get them done at a dental school. A professional dentist is supervising the students and you'll get deals of 20 to 50 percent off.

6. **Change locations.** If your child needs a procedure done and you like your doctor, ask her if she works at any other hospitals or outpatient surgery centers. Fees for different hospitals

and centers can vary by thousands of dollars, which means you can save just by asking your doctor to do the procedure elsewhere. You could save $1,000 or more by doing this.

7. **Avoid the doctor or ER when possible.** Many health plans (and some pediatricians) now have on-call nurses 24/7 that you can use free; call them to ask about a rash or a cold or something else minor (you can sometimes email them pictures) rather than paying a doctor to do it. It also may behoove you to hit up an urgent care center or a convenience care center (some drugstores have these) rather than the ER since they tend to charge far less than the ER does.

8. **Make your doctor do the hard work for you.** If you or your child is going to need a prescription, pull up the list of covered prescriptions from your insurer on your smartphone and ask the doctor to pick the best one that's the lowest cost; if you need a referral to a specialist, pull up the list of covered specialists and have your doctor pick the best one while you're sitting there. Smartphone to the rescue!

9. **Free samples.** Stock your medicine cabinet with samples from the doctor. Here's what I do, every time my daughter gets a shot, I ask for pain reliever samples in case she needs them later (she rarely does, but now I have them!) and a few extra Band-Aids. When she has the flu, I ask if they have Tylenol samples. I've stocked quite a bit of the medicine cabinet this way and I don't feel bad—the doctor is getting those samples for free anyway.

10. **Vision savings.** Skip shopping at your local vision store for glasses and contacts. You almost always find better deals online at places like ZenniOptical.com for glasses (tons of pairs for $50 or so; I just ordered a pair for $60 and adore them). For contacts, try 1800Contacts.com, as well as warehouse clubs like Sam's Club.

Momsanity Tip:

Score the First Appointment of the Day

Whether it's the doctor, pediatrician, dentist, vet, salon, or parent-teacher conference, you're often kept waiting—and that seriously eats into your day. A mom can easily waste twenty or more hours a year of her life just waiting. That's why you should try to score the first appointment of the day. At that point, no one else will have monopolized the practitioner's time, so you can get in and get out more quickly—and thus have time for yourself!

Chapter 9

Vacation

Get Away Deals

We all need to get the heck out of dodge at least sometimes. And frankly, I'm all for it: It's one of the things that makes us happiest, helps enrich our children's lives, and helps mama stay sane. I mean, there is something about your boss being hundreds of miles away—while you're watching your kids play in the ocean as you sip a fruity cocktail on the deck—that really puts life in perspective.

But there really is no need to break the bank doing it. Of course, things aren't like the good ol' days (aka your twenties)—when you'd spend weeks planning the perfect trip to Hawaii, researching every little detail from the hottest surfing instructor in Maui to the perfect spot to get fresh pineapple juice—and all of it within your budget. Now, you're lucky if you have a spare hour to plan a vacation. But this chapter is going to give you the essentials you need to know to book flights, hotels and Airbnb, a cruise, and a Disney trip without breaking the bank.

Fly for Less

You probably know to go on sites like Kayak and Google Flights (and checking the airline's site while you're at it), but here are some secrets most people don't know.

Stop listening to the book on Tuesday nonsense.

I don't know why this myth won't die, so I'm going to say it again: Tuesday afternoons are NOT always or even mostly the best time to book flights. In fact, Tuesday is only the cheapest day of the week to buy airfare for 1.6 percent of all domestic routes, according to data from flight research firm Hopper.com. That's thanks to the fact that airlines use complicated algorithms now to deal with their pricing, which means it changes all the time. Here's what to do instead: Use Hopper.com to figure out when to travel to get the best deals and/or what you should pay for a flight at any given time, and then set fare alerts using a site like Google Flights or Kayak. Simple and effective.

But do listen to the fly on Tuesday wisdom.

The cheapest two days to fly tend to be Tuesday and Wednesday, so look for flights that depart on those days to save money. An analysis by CheapAir.com found that you can save an average of $73 per ticket by flying on those days. And, in general, it tends to be more expensive to fly during the summer and cheapest to fly during January and February, though this will depend on your destination.

Know how far in advance to book.

Yes, there are last-minute deals that are ridiculously cheap, but here's the reality: On average, you'll pay an average of $150 more per ticket if you book less than two weeks ahead of when the flight takes off, as compared to those who book further out, according to data from CheapAir. So how far out should you book? That depends on where you're flying, the CheapAir data revealed. In general, book three weeks up to three and a half months ahead of the flight.

And, though these are just averages (so don't take them as strict guidelines) these are the number of days ahead of a flight you should book, depending on where you fly, according to CheapAir:

Destination	When to Book
Continental U.S. and Canada	54 days ahead
Hawaii	79 days ahead
Mexico/Central America	76 days ahead
Europe	99 days ahead
South America	81 days ahead
Asia	90 days ahead
Africa/Middle East	119 days ahead
South Pacific	89 days ahead

Remember, these won't always be the magic number—they are just helpful averages. I use these as rough guidelines and then also use Hopper's When to Fly and Buy guide and fare alerts from Google Flights or Kayak to get the cheapest tickets possible.

To avoid hassles, don't fly on a Monday.

If you want to avoid delays and cancelations—which can be both annoying and costly (entertaining the kids at the airport usually requires some serious bribery!)—don't fly on a Monday. That is the day flights are most likely to be delayed or canceled. Nearly 3 percent of flights are canceled and more than 21 percent delayed on that day, according to an analysis of Bureau of Transportation Statistics data from 2015 by aviation company Stratos Jet Charters. The reason for this isn't entirely clear, but likely has to do with the fact that it's a big day for business travel and all that congestion causes these issues.

Instead, try to go on a Saturday when only about 1 percent are canceled and 17 percent delayed. Added bonus: Security lines tend to be shorter then, too!

	Percent of flights that are canceled	Percent of flights that are delayed by 15 minutes or more
Monday	2.96 percent	21.24 percent
Tuesday	2.22 percent	19.62 percent
Wednesday	1.51 percent	18.66 percent
Thursday	1.74 percent	20.59 percent
Friday	1.12 percent	20.15 percent
Saturday	1.37 percent	17.38 percent
Sunday	1.99 percent	19.50 percent

Source: Analysis of data from the Bureau of Transportation Statistics, 2015.

Fly before 8 a.m. or after 6 p.m. to avoid delays.

If you want to avoid flight delays on whichever day you choose to fly, your best bets are to fly before 8 a.m. (the first flight of the day on your airline is the best choice) or after 6 p.m. when at least the larger airlines are more likely to have caught up from earlier delays.

Be picky about where you connect.

This sounds simple but many people forget about it when they're choosing flights. If you have to connect, don't do it through an airport like Chicago in winter, as weather is responsible for up to 70 percent of all flight delays and cancellations. Choose a sunnier, warmer weather connection destination.

Save on Where You Stay

I'm a huge fan of Airbnbs over hotels when traveling with the family because I find they save you money: The kitchen in the homes means you can make meals to save loot and often the rate for one Airbnb is cheaper than renting two hotel rooms for the fam. Plus, you can vet them for kid-friendly perks like a swing set and a yard and you get more space. But, of course, Airbnb doesn't always save you money over a hotel, and that can be particularly true in smaller towns, one study found. So this section will give you a few tips for how to rent a great hotel room or a house on the cheap.

Hotels

* **Check both the hotel website and the third-party booking sites.** I know, that's not what a busy mom wants to hear, but honestly, checking a couple booking sites and the hotel won't take you much more than 20 minutes or so. Here's the deal: Expedia, Hotels.com, Booking.com—they can all save you money, but they're not cheaper than booking right through the hotel as often as you might think. An analysis from 2017 by Piper Jaffray found that these kinds of sites had the lowest

price 21 percent of the time, the hotels themselves 13 percent of the time, and two-thirds of the time the prices were the same.

* **Sign up for price drop alerts.** Both Kayak and Hotels.com do this. Many hotels let you cancel for free within a twenty-four-hour period so what I do is book a cancelable room just so I have one, then wait to see if the price drops on a hotel I'm watching.
* **Bundle the hotel and flight.** Booking a hotel/flight package can sometimes save you 15 percent or more off the cost of your trip.
* **Use coupons and discounts.** You may not think of hotels as having coupons, but they exist. Coupons.com has a whole section of travel coupons, and a quick Google search will see if there are any coupons for the hotel or site you're trying to book. But remember my warning about coupons from page 20; be wary that you're not spending more just because you're using a coupon. It's also a good idea to see if there are employee discounts for hotels, or discounts for the military or AAA and other memberships.
* **Let the hotel know if it's a special occasion.** If it's your kid's birthday or an anniversary let the hotel know. They may give you a free upgrade or something else awesome.
* **Check out hotels in the suburbs.** Often these are cheaper per night and may have free parking (whereas parking at the hotel in the city can be pricey).

Renting a House

* **Look beyond Airbnb.** Yes, I adore Airbnb because it has so many listings at many price points, but there are other options worth considering, too. Kid & Coe lists child-friendly

properties around the globe. It's also worth looking at VRBO, HomeAway, FlipKey—and if you're short on time (who isn't!) AllTheRooms, which aggregates rooms from FlipKey, Hotels .com, Booking.com, VRBO, and more.

* **Read the reviews and ask questions.** I have stayed in dozens of Airbnbs and have rented out my place on top of that, and the biggest tip I can offer is to read the reviews on these booking sites—all of them, every word. Look for a place with at least five reviews and then read every word of them to get an idea of what the house is like beyond just the pictures and the description online. It's also worth contacting the host with questions; you will get those questions answered and also get a sense of how responsive and responsible the host really is.

* **Don't be afraid to negotiate.** If you're staying for a longer period of time, it's worth asking if there is a discount for that. Or if you're booking at the last-minute—sometimes a host will want some money rather than no money so you could get a deal by negotiating then. Just be kind and fair about this— for example on Airbnb, not only do you rate the home and the host, they rate you.

* **Consider a home swap.** While not exactly free—you typically pay a fee to list your home—this can be a way to save big on accommodations. You stay in one person's home, they stay in yours. Sites like HomeExchange.com and LoveHomeSwap .com are worth exploring for this.

Do Disney on a Dime

No doubt, you'd rather hit Cabo than spend the day with Mickey, but your kids have a totally different idea about fun—and it isn't cheap. A trip for a family of four to Disney can easily cost $5,000 or more (seriously, Cabo would be cheaper!) when you factor in tickets, airfare, and hotels. Of course, you probably know that you can cut the cost by going in the off-season like January or September instead of during school holidays (not exactly easy timing for the kids!), staying in a hotel or home outside the park, or eating outside the park. But there are plenty of lesser known and easy ways to save that don't require you to pack a lunch or stay in a crappy hotel.

The single best site for Disney savings is . . .

MouseSavers.com—it's a one-stop shop for vetted, solid Disney discounts for tickets, accommodations, and more. Definitely read their tips on what type of tickets to buy for your family—this can easily save you $100+ on tickets.

Know the common discounts.

You probably don't have time to spend hours scouring the web for coupons and other Disney savings, so let me make it easy for you. AAA members, Florida residents (for Disney World), Southern California residents (for Disneyland, sometimes), and the military can get ticket discounts, and if you work for a big company you should see if there are corporate discounts available as well (just call HR and ask).

One discount site many haven't heard of: UndercoverTourist .com, which is a discount ticket broker that has consistent deals on Disney tickets, as well as SeaWorld, LEGOLAND, and more.

Know when to go.

If possible, travel during weekdays rather than weekends. Though this can be hard with school schedules, hotels there are typically cheaper, sometimes by $100 or more a night, then. The most expensive times to hit Disney are (for the most part) when the kids are out of school (spring break, Thanksgiving, summer, et cetera). But here's a way to score a deal even when the kids are out of school: Go at the end of August (the last two weeks) if your kids start school late. Most parents don't want to vacation the week or so before school starts so there are deals to be had; get your back-to-school shopping done ahead of time and you'll have nothing to worry about.

Disney makeover for less.

If you hit up the kiddie salons in Disney World like the Bibbidi Bobbidi Boutique or the Pirates League, you'll have to fork over $60 to $200 to have your kids made over as pirates or princesses. Here's a secret: Score the kids' costumes on Amazon ahead of time and bring them with you as a surprise; these can be more comfortable than the ones at Disney anyway, and bring your own hair paint or glitter. If you plan ahead, you can score great deals on costumes right after Halloween.

Save money on food—without having to pack your own lunch.

Obviously, it's cheaper to eat outside the park than in it, but let's get real here: That requires a lot of effort that you just can't muster after a sweaty day of waiting in line for the Teacups. So here are a few ways to save on meals in the park:

○ Sign up for the email lists for a bunch of restaurants in the park about three weeks before your trip; they typically will email you coupons when you do that so you'll have plenty of saving options without having to do much work to get them.

○ Order the kid's meal—for yourself. The staff at the park often assumes you have multiple kids so they don't question it. Added bonus: You'll eat less!

○ Buy discounted gift cards. On Disney's website there is a full list of restaurants. Look to see if you can find a discounted gift card for any of them on a site like GiftCard Granny.com.

Park for free.

People who stay outside of Disney (much cheaper than staying in the resort) are often shocked at the cost of parking at the park. But here's a little-known secret: You can park for free for two hours in downtown Disney and then if you get a restaurant to validate your ticket, you can stay for an additional two. You should also look at how close your hotel is to the park; many are within walking distance, so you can save on parking that way. And ask your hotel about its shuttles to Disney.

Cruise into Savings

While a cruise isn't for everyone, they do make an easy—and affordable—family vacation. They often have plenty of activities for the kids and all of your basic meals are included (in general, the food is fine, but that's it). If you don't get sucked into the pricey extras like shore excursions and cocktails, you can take a cruise for under $100 per day per person. While you probably know some of the more obvious ways to save (like booking your own shore excursions, avoiding pricey drinks, joining the cruise line's free loyalty program and mailing list, and going in the off season), here are a few insider secrets:

Parking.

Many cruise lines charge you to park in the port—roughly $15 a day, which can add up if you take a weeklong or more cruise. Here's a trick: See if the hotel you stay in the night before the cruise (if you're planning to do this anyway) offers free parking and ask if it's okay to leave your car there; sometimes they will let you.

Unadvertised discounts.

Teachers, police, firefighters, and military may get discounts of 5 to 10 percent with a cruise line (call and ask). Plus, past passengers are often rewarded with discounts up to about 10 percent, free cabin upgrades, and more; this may apply to a cruise line's sister lines as well, so it's worth calling and mentioning that you once cruised with the line and are considering doing it again but want to know if they can give you a discount. Finally, some cruise lines offer residents of certain states savings and other perks. Join the cruise line's email list to get these deals sent right to your inbox. Get a separate email account just for promotions so they don't clog up your main email with junk. It's also worth calling a few weeks before your departure date to see if there are any discounted rooms or other upgrades available; sometimes you can get better rooms and other perks cheaply.

Time your booking right.

Two of the best times to book a cruise are between January and March (cruise lines offer tons of promotions at this time) and during Cruise Week (usually in September each year; a quick Google search will tell you the exact week, which changes each year). But here's another secret you may not know: The cruise lines are increasingly offering killer deals on Black Friday and Cyber Monday so it's worth checking on those days as well.

Where kids always sail free.

While plenty of the cruise lines offer periodic deals letting kids sail free, one little-known (but still nice) cruise line MSC Cruises, kids under eleven always sail free and kids twelve to seventeen at a reduced rate. To find all the current kids-sail-free deals, check out CruiseCompete.com—they have a special section for kids sail free deals.

Which room to book.

It can be cheaper to book two inside adjacent or nearby cabins rather than one interior family suite room. This gives you and your hubs some much-needed alone time, too! Some people hate not having a window, in which case, don't do this, but you're out of your room most of the day anyway and these cabins stay dark and are often quiet, so you get great rest. Check the deck plan (usually posted on the cruise line's website) before you book a room. Rooms under the pool deck and near the bars or nightclubs might be loud, so avoid those.

When to travel.

It's typically cheaper to cruise during hurricane season—and that also happens to be during the kids' summer vacation. While that's a little risky, the chances of your trip getting interrupted by a hurricane are low, and you can reduce them even further. First, while hurricane season is from June to November, hurricanes are most likely to hit the Eastern Caribbean from mid-August to mid-September and the Western Caribbean from mid-August through November; avoid those times if you can. The Southern Caribbean islands—Aruba, Curaçao, Trinidad and Tobago, Margarita, Bonaire—are least likely to get hit by a hurricane. In the Pacific, hurricane season is from mid-May to November but hurricanes are most likely in late August and early September. What's more, the cruise lines typically just change the itinerary to avoid a storm, so unless you had your heart set on one specific island or destination, this might not be such a big deal anyway. You can also get travel insurance to protect your investment, but don't buy it through your cruise line. Try InsureMyTrip .com. Expect to pay about 5 to 7 percent of the cost of the cruise for the policy.

Spa treatments.

If mama needs a breather from the fam, few things are as relaxing as a spa service. These aren't cheap on a cruise line (be prepared to pay upward of $120 for a massage) but there's usually one big way to save: Do your treatment on an embarkation or port day. The cruise lines have competition on these days from spas in the port. Of course, if you do your homework on the port, you can usually get one even cheaper there. Remember that gratuity is typically included in your spa service on the cruise ship so you don't need to add a tip.

Driving.

To save money and really see the destinations, get away from the awful, touristy areas right where the ships dock and avoid the too pricey and often overcrowded shore excursions by renting a car or getting a taxi to take you around. For car rentals, book weeks ahead of time and before you do it, join the (free) loyalty program of the rental car company; this is usually a good way to save money and get other perks. If you're thinking taxi, walk a bit farther from the crowded area right off the ship where lots of drivers are congregating; remember that you can negotiate with the driver, if he won't accept your deal, move on to the next driver.

Bring lots of cash.

You'll want local currency for shore outings (tips for bar tabs and spa services are typically already included, FYI), but the ATMs onboard the ships and right at the ports tend to charge high fees, so get the money before you board the ship.

Laundry.

Your kids will blow through their clothes and you might want to use the ship's laundry. If you can, wait until about the fourth day of the cruise (if it's a weeklong cruise)—that's when there is sometimes a discount involved.

Getting to your cruise.

You're well versed in finding inexpensive flights, but here's a way to get to your cruise port on the cheap that you may not have considered: Amtrak. Amtrak sometimes offers deals for cruisers to and from the port, so if you live near an Amtrak station, call and ask if it's available for you (you typically need a cruise reservation number).

Go for a repositioning cruise.

When a ship repositions—that means it moves from one port hub to another—there is typically a significant discount for riders. You get almost the same amenities you would otherwise; the big difference is you don't start and end in the same port. You can find these deals right on the cruise lines' websites, as well as the myriad cruise deal sites.

Momsanity cruise tips.

Pack a carry-on bag for you and the kids that has bathing suits in it, as well as the usual suspects like medicines, essential toiletries, passports, snacks, and a change of underwear. It can sometimes take the cruise line hours to get your bags to the room, and the kids are going to be super restless by that point because they'll have had to stand in line during the boarding process.

Buy a waterproof case for your ID, credit cards, and phone; this way, no one has to babysit your stuff while the family is at the beach in the port. While these do work most of the time, just to be safe, put your stuff in airtight plastic baggies inside the waterproof case as an extra safeguard.

Other Travel Savings Tips

* **Book car rentals online:** If you're renting a car, give the site AutoSlash.com a whirl. They will automatically apply rental car coupons to your booking, and when you enter your rental car booking info, they will tell you if another rate drops below what you paid and rebook you. I also think it's worth checking out Hotwire.com, which sometimes has great discounts.

* **When and where to rent a car:** Don't rent a car at the airport location if you can help it; their rates are nearly always pricier. And if you can rent on weekends, that tends to be cheaper, sometimes 50 percent off weekly rates. Also, if you need a car for say five or six days, check the weekly rate to see if that's less expensive than paying the daily rate for five days; often, day rates are so high that this math actually works out. Also, it's worth checking out the smaller companies like Fox, Ace, and Midway.

* **Zoo admissions for half off:** Are you a member of your local zoo? If so, you may be able to get 50 percent or more off admission into a zoo in another city. This site shows you zoos that have reciprocity with one another: www.aza.org /reciprocity.

* **Museum admission for free:** Check for free days at the museums. Many have a day when admission is free (often Mondays are popular). It's worth considering this when planning your trip. If you don't find a free day and have a Bank of America or Merrill Lynch credit or debit card, you may also get free admission. (Look on their site to see what museums participate in their program; you present your card and a photo ID and get in free.)

* **Dining out on the cheap:** If you think you'll be popping into
  a chain restaurant—even if it's just for coffee and donuts at
  Dunkin' Donuts—look for discounted gift cards for that restaurant at GiftCardGranny.com; you can sometimes save 20
  percent or more. It also sometimes pays to do your eating out
  early in the week, usually on Mondays and Tuesdays; those
  are slow days for restaurants and they often have deals. If
  you're dying to try a local restaurant, sign up for their email
  list and see if you end up with coupons or special deals sent
  to you; it's also worth checking Amazon Local, Groupon, and
  those types of sites for local deals.

Chapter 10

Saving on Everything Else

Y ou're never gonna be one of those moms who leaves Target in a huff because their diapers are just a tad more expensive this week than they were last. Frankly, you might not even notice, seeing as how your older daughter loses her mind when she sees Elsa, and Target has this irritating habit of putting the toy aisle too close to the diaper aisle. You're certainly not going out of your way to get gas that's a cent or two cheaper per gallon than at your regular spot—not with your kids demanding the Countdown Kids play on repeat. And forget about comparing whether Publix or Kroger has cheaper ketchup. You're throwing that stuff in your cart and getting the heck outta that store as fast as your yoga-pant-clad legs will carry you. No matter where you shop, you feel like this: Once you're in the store, you're committed—for better or for worse—to getting whatever it is that's on your list.

If that all sounds familiar, this chapter is for you—a mom who wants to save money, but doesn't want to have to work too hard at it. Will these rules always ensure you're getting the bargain basement price for everything you buy? Nope. To do that, you're going to have to spend hours comparison shopping and coupon hunting. In other words, this chapter is NOT—I repeat NOT—for the Coupon

Queens and Sale Slaves of the world. If you love to spend hours hunting for the lowest prices, the best sales, the most lucrative coupons, by all means, go ahead. But if you don't have the time or patience to spend more than a few minutes bargain hunting, scouring for coupon codes, or price comparing on a bunch of websites, read on for big rules of thumb that will generally save you money in minimal time.

3 Super Quick Online Money-Saving Hacks

Beyond sites like Ebates to get cash back when you shop, most moms I know don't really do anything else. Here are three programs I love that you might not have heard of. You can download each of these browser extensions and apps in under a minute for free, and then, when you're shopping online, they'll pop up automatically and help you shop better.

   1. **Honey:** When you're shopping for something, Honey finds coupons for the site you're on and automatically applies them to your order when you check out. Will it save you a ton? Not usually, but a few bucks here and there sure—and since it requires almost no time on your end (no searching for coupons, it's all automatic), I'm all for it!

   2. **PriceBlink:** It automatically tells you via a bar at the top of the page if there's a lower price on an item you're looking at on another site and lets you compare online reviews. I've saved quite a bit using this program! (InvisibleHand works like PriceBlink and I like that one, too.)

   3. **Paribus:** I have gotten $50+ back by using this site! When you buy something from a number of retailers (including Walmart

and Target, which I know many moms use all the time), it automatically checks if the price dropped within the retailer's price protection period. If it did, Paribus automatically contacts the retailer to refund you the difference between what you paid and the new lower price.

When to Shop for Everything

If you're like me, you don't have time to constantly search for sales. So this section will tell you when pretty much everything you might want to buy tends to be on sale. In general, the number one best month to shop if you're looking for deals is January, as stores try to drum up at least some business during the postholiday bonanza.

But really, when to get the best deals depend on what you're buying. I asked my friends over at Adobe—which has eight years of sales data from 4,500 companies and 55 million products (that's a lot of knowledge!)—to run some custom numbers to help us know, definitively, when the best time to buy certain things online is. Here are some of the pricey things moms buy, when to buy them—and how much timing your shopping can save you.

You need:	Buy it in:	Average discount (as compared to the average month)
Appliance	November	7.01 percent
Computer	December	7.35 percent
Tablet	December	12.88 percent
TV	November	14.73 percent

You need:	Buy it in:	Average discount (as compared to the average month)
Other electronics	November	6.99 percent
Furniture and bedding	November	2.8 percent
Toys	November	5.37 percent
Sports Equipment	November	5.05 percent
Flights	January	8.28 percent
Hotels (in the U.S.)	December	6.56 percent
Over-the-counter medication	September	0.46 percent

Source: Adobe.

Finding deals on clothing is all about timing as well: Once an item has lingered on the shelves for six weeks or more, the retailer is likely to mark it down to try to sell it. That's why it's a bad idea to buy seasonal clothing early in the season.

Where to (and Not to) Shop

Want to know what kinds of things to buy at X store and what other kinds of things to buy at Y store, so that you'll generally save money? This is the section for you.

It's almost never a good idea to buy things at the drugstore; the drugstore is convenient, but typically expensive. Yes, there are sometimes deals and sales, especially if you're a member of the loyalty program, but, in general, unless you're a diligent sale-hunter, you are better off shopping elsewhere. The same is true of the grocery store (see page 22). Costco and HealthWarehouse.com tend to have the best deals on your family's prescriptions. For over-the-counter meds, try the warehouse clubs and Target and Walmart. Buy pregnancy tests at the dollar store; their tests may be slightly less sensitive than a pricey test but once you're a day or two past a missed period, they will be able to give you an accurate result, too.

In general, don't shop at stores with "baby" (or similar) in the name. This is like saying the word "wedding" when you're shopping for wedding stuff—it immediately means you may pay way more. Buy your baby gate online in the pet department. Seriously, the doggie gate will keep your child in the playroom just as well as the child gate will; you don't have to tell anyone you did this! It's the same thing usually, but costs less. Don't buy diapers at a kids' or baby store, either; Amazon—with Subscribe & Save feature + Amazon Family—or Costco (and other big box retailers), Walmart, or Target are usually the way to go here. High chairs and other gear are usually better bets at Ikea and Amazon. Of course, there will be exceptions to these "rules" but in general if you follow them, you're likely to save money.

How to Shop the Low-Cost Stores Smartly

By now, you know shopping for secondhand goodies, and at places like Costco, Sam's, Target, Walmart, and Amazon can save you money. But here are some of the secrets to shopping at these places smartly (without having to scour coupons and sales).

* **The Warehouse Clubs (Costco, Sam's, et cetera):** Since you know you can get great deals on everything from food to towels at these spots, rather than telling you what TO buy there (most things are decent deals), I'm going to tell you what NOT to buy. Don't buy:
  * Books—Amazon and Barnes & Noble are almost always a better deal.
  * Condiments—they usually come in such large quantities that they expire before you use them up unless you've got a super big family or entertain a lot.
  * Sunscreen—look at its expiration date if you buy here to make sure it won't go to waste.
  * Clothes and shoes—often the quality is lacking.
* **Big-Box Stores (Target, Walmart, et cetera):** Like the warehouse clubs, these obviously offer great deals on tons of things from snack foods to cleaning supplies to clothes. So let's look at what NOT to buy at these stores. Don't buy:
  * Furniture—it's cheap but often not great quality; try a Home Goods–type store instead.
  * Prescription drugs—warehouse clubs tend to be slightly cheaper.
  * Wrapping paper and other holiday items—the dollar store will often be even cheaper.
  * Books—go for Amazon or Barnes & Noble.
* **Toy Stores:** As we talk about on page 161, I am a BIG fan of getting almost all of your toys secondhand. Still, I know at times you can't resist a trip to the toy store. As I'm sure you long ago figured out, boutique toy stores tend to be priciest, and the big toy store chains tend to have slightly better prices on toys. Target and Walmart are also great spots for buying toys. In general, do NOT buy things like diapers, batteries,

and party supplies at the toy store—these tend to be way more expensive there than elsewhere.

* **Amazon:** There's no shame in knowing the UPS guy's name and life story—Amazon is legit cheaper than other stores for a bunch of items. An analysis of 52,000 products in 13 categories by Profitero found that, in general, Amazon was cheaper than Walmart, Target, and Jet.com; Walmart was the closest in terms of price (at about 3 percent more). And according to an analysis of 1,500 products Savings.com did, which compared Amazon prices to prices from dozens of other online stores including the big-box chains, Amazon tends to offer the best deals on inexpensive things for under $10 (the cheap stuff on Amazon is usually really cheap), and bulk items like diapers and wipes, especially if you're a Prime and Amazon Family member. But Amazon is not the best place to get good deals on a few items.

Don't buy:
- ○ Clothing and shoes
- ○ Beauty products—the Profitero study found that Walmart has slightly cheaper prices than Amazon on beauty items.
- ○ Cleaning supplies

If you order roughly three or more items per month on Amazon, the $99 Prime membership is probably worth your while; Profitero found that roughly three out of four of the most popular products on Amazon were available for Prime shipping. And here's something else moms should know: Products on Amazon change price an average of 4.6 times over the course of the month, and some change multiple times per day (usually a max of about twenty-eight times per month). That means that consumers who can wait to get something should check the items they want a few times a week (if they have time) to score the lowest price, or simply set up a price alert online.

Beware of Amazon's Subscribe & Save, yes, it's convenient and gives you a discount, but the item may have changed in price since the last time you bought it, meaning it's no longer a good deal. Because you automatically order the item with Subscribe & Save, you are forced into paying the sometimes higher price.

Also, Prime members have to be aware of what I call the "Prime trap"—the fact that just being a member of Prime can make you spend more. One study found that Prime members spend more than double what non-Prime members do on Amazon. And if you think about it, that makes sense—you need something, you know you get free shipping on Amazon, so you don't bother to look elsewhere for the product.

Want to know if you're getting the best price on Amazon? Check out CamelCamelCamel.com, which tracks that for thousands of Amazon items.

Quick Tip

Get the family's hair cut at beauty schools rather than salons (check out LocalBeautySchools.com to find one near you); the students are supervised by a pro and typically services are a fraction of the cost.

Savings Tips for Expectant or Brand-new Moms

1. **Go ahead and cheap out on the crib.** Oh sure, we all dream of a gorgeous Stokke crib, but it's kind of crazy to spend a ton here. All cribs sold in the U.S. have to meet federal safety standards, spending more money doesn't get you a safer crib, just one with more bells and whistles (better finishes, materials, et cetera). Since your child will grow out of this crib in a few years, it just doesn't make sense to spend a ton. But don't buy cribs used. Even if the crib was bought a few years ago, one missing or severely stripped screw, and your baby could get hurt. Though the idea seems practical, you don't want to pay extra for a crib that will convert into a toddler bed; most kids can go from the crib to a twin bed without needing the toddler bed—if you time it right.

2. Walmart, Ikea, and Amazon have cribs starting at around $150 that will last long enough (I bought mine from Amazon and it's been great!). Check out the crib you want in store by looking at the display model; jiggle it and examine the materials to assess quality. Do this before placing an online order because it's a pain in the butt to ship a crib that you don't want back to the manufacturer, even if the company offers free returns. Beware: Most mattresses are sold separately (and you don't need a super fancy one! No frills works just fine).

3. **Little kids often don't care about the price tag.** I once read something about parenting that still rings true to me today: The amount your kid likes whatever it is you bought him is inversely related to the price. This has been true about 70 percent of the time in my house (at least in my daughter's younger years!). I bought her an ExerSaucer with

all the bells and whistles. I know, I know—I should, and do, know better! But we all make mistakes (especially after a tantrum-filled rainy day where you're stuck inside!). She HATED it. Meanwhile, her favorite plaything was the Baby Einstein toy someone had bought us off her registry. During their first year of life, it seems most kids like the wrapping paper more than the gifts! That taught me something important, though: When there's an item at a range of different prices—like say bottles or sheets or sippy cups—scour those reviews before you buy the expensive version. I know it sounds simple, but it's one of the main rules I follow in my house. Most likely, you can find a generic or used version of the expensive item, and your child will never know the difference.

4. **Use a Pack 'n Play instead of a bassinet.** Instead of buying a bassinet for your baby to sleep in your room for the first few months, buy a Pack 'n Play and put the baby in that next to your bed; you'll use this later when you travel, anyway.

5. **Buy a dresser that can double as a changing table.** Just add an inexpensive contouring changing pad to the top, which can be found for less than $20. By buying one instead of two separate pieces of furniture, you can often cut your furniture costs in half. If you're having trouble resisting the pricey furniture—everything from the crib to the dresser—think of it like this: You can easily save $500 by furnishing your nursery with just the basics; put that $500 into your kid's college savings plan (assuming a 5 percent annual rate of return, which is pretty standard)—and never add another dime to it—and you'll have more than $1,200 for her to go to college in eighteen years! Not bad!

6. **Use a booster seat that straps onto a chair.** These often cost just around $30, versus buying a high chair, which can cost

$100 and up. Bonus: You'll want one of these to take with you when you travel, anyway.

7. **Don't overspend on the car seat.** Parents dump big bucks on car seats, sometimes spending upward of $300 on one. But like a crib, all car seats sold in the U.S. must meet federal safety standards, so spending more doesn't necessarily get you a safer car seat. *Consumer Reports* is a simple, trustworthy go-to to compare car seats' functionality, safety, and price. I subscribe, and find that the online access is worth the money every single year. They often recommend safe and functional car seats that may cost as little as about $50, like the Cosco Scenera NEXT. Amazon often has great deals on car seats, as do Target and Walmart.

8. **Don't overthink diaper shopping.** You can find great diaper deals at places like Target, Walmart, the warehouse clubs like Sam's and Costco, and on Amazon—one day one might have the best deal, another day another will. There isn't one place that always has the lowest prices, so don't drive yourself crazy looking. The big no-no when it comes to buying diapers are the grocery store and the drugstore—those two places often charge a premium (sometimes up to 10 cents more *per diaper*) and rarely have the lowest prices.

Savings Tips for Moms with Older Kids

At this point, you're pretty savvy about a lot of your spending—after all you've got at least a couple years of parenting under your belt! And you definitely know how to say no to a kid—even when they're in full-whine mode in a crowded store! But I'm going to talk about a few of the spending traps that even experienced moms find themselves in—and what to do about it.

Beware of the "present pressure" during the holidays.

Many moms I know feel immense pressure to make the holidays perfect for their children—including buying all the gifts they want, which costs a ton—and this stresses them out. So what can you do about it? The rule here is simple: Happiness matters most (but don't forget that iPad!). Here's what I mean by that: In the age of social media where you can see what every other mom has bought her kids for the holidays, it's hard not to get swept up in the present-buying pressure. Most of us do: Parents spend an average of $271 per child on holiday gifts, with one in ten saying they spend $500 or more per child, a 2011 survey from *Today* Parents and Parenting .com showed.

But if you only remember one thing this holiday season, remember this: Studies on what makes people happy show that it's experiences, not things, that drive lasting happiness. And isn't that what you really want for your children? At least eight studies on the topic confirm that while that brand new iPad may initially elate your kids, that joy wanes pretty quickly. On the flip side, a positive holiday experience of fun, laughter, and love with the family breeds lasting contentment.

I can hear you groaning right now because while that all sounds wonderful, your kids are going to FREAK when they don't get that iPad. So here's a smart way to handle it. Give the kids one (just one!) big present from mom and dad and drastically cut out the other little things that you often get them, which add up. Instead, use that extra money to plan a fun activity for the whole family. It doesn't even have to be pricey. A sleigh ride, making a gingerbread house together at home—whatever it is, something that you think your kids will enjoy and that you can all do together. And to stop your guilt at them only having a few presents to open, think back to your own childhood—you probably remember that one "great" gift you got each year (for me it was the Nintendo on Christmas morning—have I dated myself enough yet?), but I doubt you remember all the other ones; that was money your parents dropped down the drain.

Grinchy but Great: Negotiate a "Gift Truce" with Adult Friends and Family

For 99.9 percent of us, it's not really an option to not get the kids gifts during the holidays—but what about adult friends and family? That's more flexible. Just ask forty-seven-year-old Michelle Morton, of Raleigh, N.C., who I interviewed for MarketWatch on this topic. She, her sisters, and her husband don't exchange gifts with one another. "It was stressful and expensive getting all those gifts, when none of us really needed any of it," she told me. For a while, she felt like they were all just getting each other gift cards and it didn't feel very meaningful. Now, instead of gifts, they all fly up to visit her parents in upstate New York—and that's the way she plans to keep it.

If you're sitting here reading this and calling me "the Grinch" in your head, you're not alone. Some people can't stomach this idea. But others that I talked to said they loved the freedom of not having to do much holiday shopping—and the pressure to get the perfect gift. If this sounds tempting to you, start by having a conversation with friends and family about not getting gifts this year, or at least about setting monetary limits on gifts: Feel them out on the issue. You can best sell the idea by thinking about what kind of pitch would most appeal to the person. For your cheapskate father, push the financial angle; for your hippie sister, the eco-friendly angle; for your stressed-out brother, the time-saving angle.

Stop falling into the new toy trap.

It's all about the parent guilt here—your kid wants the latest and greatest, and you go and get it. In general, you don't need to buy many toys new. Some of the exceptions to that rule are bike and scooter helmets (they may have been in an accident), bath toys (those can get moldy fast), and stuffed animals (they can have allergens and even lice); think about safety when you're thinking new or used. If it's a safe toy that can easily be cleaned before giving it to your kids, why buy it new? Just get some antibacterial wipes, or good old soap and water, and wash the toy down. Need a reminder that I'm right about buying toys used? Look around at all the toys in your house now that your child barely ever plays with; I'm guessing very few were worth the sticker price.

I know, you're groaning and thinking: But popping into Toys "R" Us and loading up is so easy! Um, counterpoint: So is shopping on eBay and Amazon, both of which have used toys that can cut your costs in half, as do consignment shops. Better yet: Sometimes you can score free toys—sign up for mommy groups and Listservs in your area (I've gotten a ton here), look on Freecycle.com or "buy nothing" groups, or just ask friends and family if they have something to get rid of. If you're motivated (and have the time) a toy swap works, too; have your mom friends come over and each bring five toys, have a few glasses of wine, and trade accordingly. You can also check out sites like Swap.com.

Momsanity Advice

Q: When does my generosity cross the line into spoiling my kids?

A: The answer to this is, surprisingly, less about how many things you buy than it is about how the kids react to and feel about those things. "It's about gratitude," says Elizabeth Lombardo, author of *Better than Perfect: 7 Strategies to Crush Your Inner Critic and Create a Life You Love*, who has seen many rich people with nearly every toy at their fingertips who are nevertheless well adjusted and feel incredibly grateful for what they have. It's okay to keep giving to a child who feels grateful for what she gets; not a good idea to keep giving to a child who feels entitled to the things she gets. How do you teach gratitude? Of course, you can tell them about it, but the best way for kids to learn gratitude is for their parents to model it for them often. Have them watch you thank others daily for everything from bagging your groceries to washing your car, make a ritual where you both nightly share what you are grateful for, bring gifts to others like the pediatrician for no reason (have the kids help make the gifts), and make volunteering and giving back to your community a regular part of your household. It's also essential that your kids understand—and appreciate—all the hard work that went into you paying for and getting the things you give them. Talk to them about work, what that means for you, what it entails, and about how others are less fortunate but that they can do something about this.

So how do you know if your kids might be entitled? It's sometimes hard to see it when you're in the thick of it, but there are some phrases that your kids say that can signal to you that they feel entitled to things rather than grateful for them. These are big red flags that you may be spoiling them. If you hear "I deserve X" (as in, "Mom, I deserve a new iPad because I've done so well in school"), or if when you ask your kids why they want something, they say something like "because other kids at school have it" or "because I want it," you should take these as warning signs that you haven't communicated fully to your kids that the physical things they get from you like toys and electronics are a privilege, not a right. Yes, at one time or another, almost every one of our kids will say something like this so don't feel bad! Instead, use it as a moment to highlight your family's values. Kids should feel grateful that you can and do buy them things, not that they are entitled to things just because other people have them or because they've done something to deserve them or even just because they want them.

Part II

A Mom's Guide to Getting Her Finances Under Control in 30 Minutes a Week

Part II

Chapter 11

You Don't Have to Be an Investing Whiz to Build a Solid Nest Egg

I write about personal finance for a living—and I, too, have failed at sticking to a budget. When I had my daughter, my expenses were almost immediately higher but my husband and my income had not budged. Though I'd successfully stayed on a budget many times in my life, with my daughter and a full-time job, I was so busy, and the old ways of budgeting were no longer cutting it. I will say this, though: It was a great learning experience, because I had to rethink the kind of budget that would work for me.

Some of the advice out there has you on a monthly budget. You figure out what you can spend each month, then go about your daily life buying things and paying bills. At the end of the month, you look at what happened over that month to make sure you stayed on track. That became a problem fast when my daughter was born because I was busy with her, I'd often spend without thinking (desperate late-night baby-won't-sleep Amazon purchases, impromptu snacks or treats for her, et cetera). I'd spend and forgot I did it—which wasn't doing any favors for my bottom line. For me (and most moms I know), MOM BRAIN IS REAL! Mostly, it's because we have our own lives and one little life—or two or three—to take care of, too; our brains are overloaded! Plus, the little expenses of having a kid add up. You don't necessarily think you're spending a lot more, but you get your bills and nearly keel over. So that whole "monthly check-in" thing wasn't cutting it. I mean, what if you only weighed yourself once a month; do you really think you'd be able to stick to a diet? Um, no! Need those bursts of motivation each week.

Once I figured out that whole monthly budget thing wasn't working, I tried to overcompensate by looking at my spending every day, which I'd also read was *the* way to do it. But that was kind of like staying on a diet where you have to count every calorie. For a couple weeks or so, you meticulously do it, certain that this will (finally!) be the time you lose the mommy muffin top once and for all. But then, a mere week or so later, you find yourself elbows deep in the Ben & Jerry's and think, *I cannot do this* and give up on the strict dieting entirely. Same with money: Too strict = makes you cray. So the daily budget fizzled fast—this busy mom was always forgetting to check her spending! I needed more frequent money check-ins than once a month, but I couldn't rely on myself to check in with my spending every day. Plus, when I did check in on my spending I needed it to be *brief*; it had to fit into my schedule of playdates and activities and the nightly half hour I get to actually see how my husband's day went. It also had to be simple—no meticulous adding and subtracting, no figuring out how much I had left to pay bills versus all the fun extras I wanted to buy my daughter. It had to ensure I was building a solid financial future for my family with savings and paying down debts. Oh, and (man do I have a lot of requirements!) my budget had to accommodate at least the occasional splurge. Without that, this whole plan was too much.

It took some time and experimentation, but I found a reasonable plan that works within a busy mom's real life. Rather than creating a monthly or daily budget, you're going to create a smart, adaptable weekly one that simply divides your spending into two categories so you can more easily keep track of it. That's what I'll show you how to do in Chapters 12–19. It will take some legwork to create your customized plan, but once you do, you only need to spend about thirty minutes a week dealing with your finances. As part of that legwork you will learn how to smartly tackle what I call the "Money-Savvy Mama's Quick Guide"—which contains the five things every mom needs to do to get on the right financial track and is short enough to fit on a three-by-three-inch Post-it note. Really, it's just five—some financial experts try to overcomplicate this, but I'm not having it!

The Money-Savvy Mama's Quick Guide

The 5 things you need to do to get your finances on track.

- Manage your basic living costs
- Smartly pay down your debt
- Get the right insurance
- Build up emergency savings
- Save for periods of financial freedom (and eventual retirement)

Is this freaking you out because you've never been that great at financial stuff? I know plenty of women who think that dealing with their finances—especially things like investing or insurance policies—is something they're never going to be good at. I've met them, I've talked to them, and, in fact, I used to be one of them.

I moved to New York in my twenties from Texas with pretty much zero knowledge about how to handle my finances. My first course of action was to get a studio apartment that ate up way too much of my paycheck. My second course of action was to get pretty friendly with my credit card so that I could at least try to look as hip as the thin, well-dressed women swirling around me every day. I'd see the credit card bills each month, but they barely phased me; I could, after all, afford the minimum payments.

Then I got a wake-up call. I got promoted to be the financial marketing manager at *Forbes* magazine—and I knew pretty much zero about finance beyond that if I got fired from said job, I was in deep doo-doo! I remember being in a meeting where they were all talking about Roth IRAs and I was nodding authoritatively like, "yeah, Roth IRA." I had no clue what they were talking about. I had to run back to my desk and google it! Slowly but surely, I began to learn about finance, and I transformed my financial situation. I got out of credit card debt, I began socking away 12 percent of my income for retirement, I built up an emergency savings fund.

In doing that I realized getting on the right financial footing isn't as hard as many experts make it out to be. You don't have to become an investing whiz to build a solid nest egg. In fact, the rules of investing are pretty simple. You don't have to live like a pauper to get out of debt, either. Though admittedly, that Gilt habit will probably need to get whittled down to more of an occasional indulgence.

Now that I'm a mom, I realize that having a solid nest egg, emergency savings, and the right insurance is more important than ever. There is someone else depending on me now, so it's essential that I have a cushion of savings built up. Should I lose my job, we could still afford our mortgage, groceries, and car until I found other work. It's crucial that I have life and disability insurance so that if something happened to me, she would be taken care of financially until she was old enough to support herself. It's essential that I have enough saved for retirement so she isn't forced to have me live with her (and pay for my care) in my old age because I can't afford to live on my own. No one wants their mom and dad—even if they love them to pieces—living with them when they have their own kids to deal with!

Frankly, having a secure financial footing is one of the most important gifts you can give your kids—and it's far less difficult than you might think. The following chapters are going to show you how to deal with each of those five things I mentioned in a simple way. For each item, I'm going to give you some "legwork" to do so you can begin handling each smartly. This "legwork" may take you some time (I know, not what you wanted to hear, but I'm going to break it into manageable tasks for you!).

Don't worry, each item shouldn't take you more than a few hours, and when it does, I'll show you how to easily do it in steps or how you can outsource the task. This budget plan will get you and your family on a solid financial footing, helping you quickly pay down debts, build up savings, and pay for your essentials like housing and food. It will also allow you to have fun with your money (life, after all, isn't worth living without a little fun!). Once you do this work, it's smooth sailing, and Chapter 18 is going to show you how you can spend the money you have left over—your (mostly) play money!—to maximize your and your family's happiness (hello beach vacation!). Then Chapter 17 ties this all together. It's where you're going to learn how to manage all of your money in about thirty minutes a week to ensure your family remains on solid financial ground and has money to continue to enjoy life's little pleasures!

Chapter 12

The Smart Way to Manage Your Basic Living Costs

E ach month, everyone must pay for their basic living costs like food, shelter (plus insurance to protect it), and clothing (and I do mean basic here!), as well as utilities (water, phone, gas, electricity, et cetera), health care premiums, in most cases a car with insurance and gas, and a few other things. I consider these the starter kit to an adult life. Yes, you could live without a phone or a car, but for most of us, that makes modern life nearly impossible. In this chapter, I'm going to walk you through what's included in your basic bills and how to start tracking them.

The Money-Savvy Mama's Quick Guide

The 5 things you need to do to get your finances on track.

- **Manage your basic living costs**
- Smartly pay down your debt
- Get the right insurance
- Build up emergency savings
- Save for periods of financial freedom (and eventual retirement)

We're going to start with a system to deal with all those basic bills and costs that will make it super easy to manage. Don't panic: This may seem overwhelming at first, but everything will be clearly and easily explained so you'll have your finances under control in no time!

What Are Your Basic Bills?

The first thing you must, must do is take care of the basics you need to live. And by basics, I do mean basic! Basics include:

* Food
* Essential clothing
* Housing
* Home insurance
* Utilities (phone, internet, water, gas, electric, trash)
* Car
* Car insurance
* Gas
* Medicine
* Health insurance
* Childcare, if you need to work
* Basic school supplies for the kids
* Essential toiletries

Basics may also include essential car and home maintenance like regular oil changes, HOA fees, work commuting costs, taxes you pay out of pocket, and alimony or child support, among other things essential to your life. Basics do not include a massage at the spa or that really cute dress, no matter how much you want and deserve one, or both! Nor do they include a date-night sitter or premium television and streaming services. I'm not saying you can't have these things, of course. We'll certainly get to that. But we have to start with the things you absolutely need; determine your bare minimum cost of living. We'll also tackle credit card bills in the next chapter when we look at debt.

Step 1: Know What You're Spending

The first thing you must do to deal with all your living costs is to list them. Fill in the chart below with what you owe each month, the highest amounts you've paid over the past year, and, if applicable, when the bill is due (e.g., first of the month, every three months, et cetera). If you pay for your essential clothes or groceries using your credit card, use your credit card due date.

If your monthly bill is not a fixed amount, find the average using bank or credit card statements for the past year, adding up the last twelve months, then dividing by twelve. For insurance, break down into a cost per month rather than annually or biannually, as it is charged. For anything you pay for irregularly in cash or by debit card, you can leave the due date blank.

In some instances, you might combine categories, and that's fine. For example, if you buy essential toiletries with your groceries (even though supermarkets aren't the best deals, see page 22), you can include them with food rather than list them separately.

This whole process could take you six hours or more; so here's how to tackle it over the course of seven to eight days in about an hour per day. Don't have an hour each day? Just break each day into two days (so this will take you two weeks instead of one) and take your time doing this. And remember, after you do this legwork, you will soon be managing your money in just thirty minutes a day!

Day 1: The easy stuff. Start with the items that you tend to pay the same amount on each month or semi-regularly like your mortgage/rent, insurance (car, life, home, disability, health), phone, car, and internet service and fill those amounts in. A quick look at your online bank account should tell you how much you paid on those. (Skip any bill that is not about the same each month, we'll deal with those later.) Do NOT include items that are automatically deducted from your paycheck like health, disability, and life insurance. If you pay an item like an insurance bill twice a year, break this out into monthly installments by dividing the annual cost by twelve. *Estimated time: 1 hour.*

Days 2 and 3: Groceries. Look back at your credit card and bank statements over the past year and do your best to determine how much you spent on groceries for each of the past twelve months. It's easy to do this by logging into your online accounts, and it might make sense to print all credit card and bank statements out and highlight grocery bills in a certain color so it's easy to do; write down the total each month on each statement. (Some credit cards and banks break out your spending by category so this can be an even easier way to find your grocery spending.) Note the month when you spent the most and average the amounts for the rest of the year. If you can't find statements for a full year, just do the best you can with statements you do have.

Estimated time: 1 to 4 hours.

Day 4: Utilities. Do the same as you did for groceries for gas, water, and electricity bills. This tends to be relatively easy to look through because you only pay these bills once a month. Usually the payment is reflected both in past utility bills (see if you can access these online) and your online bank account. *Estimated time: 1 to 2 hours.*

Day 5: Other health care costs and gas. Repeat what you did for groceries here. Other health care costs would include things like regular copays and medicines. *Estimated time: 1 to 3 hours.*

Day 6: Essential clothing and toiletries. Repeat what you did for groceries here. Essential toiletries include things like toilet paper, toothpaste, tampons, soap, et cetera. Essential clothing is anything that a member of your family couldn't manage without. For example, your child needs new shirts if the old ones don't fit anymore, not because they now really love unicorns. *Estimated time: 1 to 2 hours.*

Day 7: Childcare and basic school supplies. For those with a regular sitter or nanny or regular daycare this should be pretty simple to estimate, but it can be harder if, say, you paid a sitter who came at irregular times in cash, so do what you can here. For school supplies, repeat what you did for groceries here; most of your spending on these items was likely in July/August so knowing that should make it easier. *Estimated time: 1 to 2 hours.*

Day 8: If there is any other bill that is essential to your life, include it here. Do not include things automatically deducted from your paycheck. Also, if say your phone or another bill is in an irregular amount each month, so it didn't get included in your Day 1 plan, do that on this day. *Estimated time: 1 to 2 hours.*

What I Spend Each Month on My Bills

	Amount Owed Each Month		Day Due
	Average	Highest	
Groceries			
Mortgage or rent			
Gas (home)			
Water			
Electricity			
Trash			
Phone			
Car payment			
Gas (car)			
Internet			

	Amount Owed Each Month		Day Due
	Average	Highest	
Home or renter's insurance			
Car insurance			
Life insurance			
Disability insurance			
Childcare			
Health insurance			
Other health costs			
Essential clothing			
Essential toiletries			
Basic school supplies			
Taxes			
Other:			
Other:			

Step 2: Reduce Your Costs

Now that you've looked at all your costs, did you notice some of them are higher than you realized? I want you to make sure you're not spending more than you need to on these items and make cuts when you need to. Refer back to Part I for ways to save. For example, Chapters 3 and 6 can help you determine if your car and homeowners insurance bills are too high, and gives other ways to cut your bills; Chapter 8 can help with health care and health insurance; Chapter 5 can help with childcare.

So now that you know what your costs are, is there a better way to handle paying for them? Yes! But we're going to get to that later. For now, just keep paying these bills as you usually do. In Chapter 17, I'm going to give you an easy way to stay on top of your bills, including automating many of the bills that you don't already have automated.

Help! I Can't Pay All My Bills

Something happens—you lose your job, you get hit with a huge bill—and you realize you won't be able to pay the minimums on all your bills. What do you do?

1. **Focus on what's important.** Start by paying your basic necessities that we just established, like food, utilities, health care, a car if you need it to get to work, a roof over your head, and what you owe the government (i.e., taxes).
2. **Tackle your federal student loans.** Look into repayment options that might work for you, like those based on income or financial hardship (StudentAid.ed.gov gives details); this can dramatically lower payments and free up cash for other debts.
3. **Deal with other debts like credit cards.** You should also always pay the minimums (and of course, ideally more) on your debts. Move a balance to another low-interest card if you need to; if you're late on payments, call your credit card company and explain that you will not be able to pay the full minimum; see if they can give you a repayment option that is less than what you have now. Sites like Bankrate.com can help you navigate this situation.

If things get really bad, consider seeing a credit counselor, who can create a plan to manage these debts for you. There are some scams out there, so look for an organization that is a nonprofit and a member of the National Foundation of Credit Counseling (go to NFCC.org to find options in your area). Make sure that organization is a member of the Better Business Bureau and has no complaints against it. Some universities, military bases, and credit unions operate nonprofit credit counseling programs. Before you hire anyone, interview the person to make sure they are legit. You can find questions to ask and other information at Consumer.ftc.gov.

Momsanity Tip: Keep Bill-Paying Sane by Opening an Email Account Just for Your Bills

The easiest way I know to eliminate all your financial clutter is to get all of your bills sent to one exclusive email address. This may require changing your preferences from paper to email or creating a new email address and changing it on all your accounts. But it's worth the effort when it simplifies your life (all bills in one place), keeps bills and other financials separate from work and personal emails, and prevents all those important papers from cluttering up your countertops.

Momsanity Advice

Q: How do I deal with "mom guilt" brought on by not having the money to buy the kids what they want?

A: Beverly Hills–based family and relationship psychotherapist Fran Walfish, who has treated hundreds of children and their parents, said it best: "When children grow up and become adults and end up on my couch, they don't complain about what gifts their parents did or didn't get them." Nope, they complain about things like not getting enough attention or love, she says. How spot on she is. Material wealth has little impact on children's happiness, revealed a 2009 study of more than 50,000 children in fifteen countries, which asked children about their friendships, living situation, money, family, school life, and more. Indeed, children in affluent Norway were as happy as children in Nepal and Algeria. What's more, Romanian children—not among the world's richest by any means—were happiest followed by those in Colombia and Israel. In short: Stop feeling guilty about the things you can't afford to buy your kids; those things aren't going to make them happier. Then, remember this: "Stuff doesn't make us happier, relationships do, experiences do," says psychologist Elizabeth Lombardo. It's far more important for you to spend time with your kids, do activities with them, nurture them, than it ever will be to buy them the gadgets and things that they want. Yes, they will whine—possibly even tell you that you are ruining their life—but this is short-lived, while the love you give them and the time you spend with them lasts forever. Take that, money guilt!

Chapter 13

An Easy Guide to Paying Down Debt

D-E-B-T: It's the four-letter word most of us need to face up to—and it comes in a lot of forms: Mortgages, credit cards, student loans, personal loans, and more. It also often comes with a huge downside (besides its high cost). People with high levels of debt have higher levels of stress and depression and are in worse health than those who don't, according to a recent study published in the journal *Social Science & Medicine*. And frankly, being stressed out or depressed and in rough health will impact your kids. This is not at all meant to make you feel guilty about your debt, or add to your stress. It is only meant to encourage you to do something about it, if not for yourself, then for them! So let's look at how to get a handle on what debts you owe and how to tackle them smartly.

The Money-Savvy Mama's Quick Guide

The 5 things you need to do to get your finances on track.

- Manage your basic living costs
- **Smartly pay down your debt**

- Get the right insurance
- Build up emergency savings
- Save for periods of financial freedom (and eventual retirement)

People with debt fall into two groups: 1) those with high-interest debt (anything over about 6 to 7 percent like credit card debt); and 2) those without high-interest debt. Let's start with a general overview for how to tackle both high-interest and low-interest debt, then we'll get into a more detailed plan.

If you DO have high-interest debt, start by doing all of these three things:

1. Pay down as much as you can on your high-interest debt, like credit card debt, each month.
2. Pay the minimums on all other debts.
3. Put up to what your employer matches (if they do, in fact, match) into your 401(k), but not more.

Not sure how much more you can pay toward your credit card each month? One simple rule is to aim to spend a specific amount less each week—say $25 or $50 a week—and put that toward your credit card; see how that feels after the first month and keep upping it if needed. I also like using Bankrate.com's credit card calculator, which you can find on their site. You enter the amount of debt you have and when you'd like to have it paid off, and it will tell you what you need to spend each month to make it happen. Once you've knocked that credit card debt out, take some time to celebrate, and proceed to the next section.

If you DON'T have high-interest debt, here's what you should focus on:

1. Building up your emergency fund (see page 203).
2. Saving enough for retirement (13 to 15 percent of your income).
3. Paying down your lower interest debts.

If you're not on track with retirement savings, try to get there before you start quickly paying down a low-interest debt, like a 3.5 percent mortgage. You'll likely earn more over the long-term in your retirement account (the average is about 6 percent annually) than the mortgage rate costs you. Once you're on track with retirement savings (see page 212 for how much you should have saved), you can work on saving for your child's college and other goals.

How Credit Card Interest Works

Let's say you have a credit card with a 15 percent APR, which stands for "annual percentage rate." This is the interest rate your card is charging you. But the company won't just tack on 15 percent at the end of the year and charge you that. Instead, most charge interest each day. To figure out what you're charged each day, divide that APR by 365, which in this case comes out to 0.041 percent each day; that's the interest you're charged a day. So, if you had a $1,000 balance, your balance for the end of the day would be $1,000.41. Of course, if you keep buying things, the interest gets charged on those things, too, each day. If you don't spend on anything else, you'll end up with a balance of roughly $1,013 at the end of the month.

   Now let's look at how interest can get out of control. Interest on a credit card compounds—and you're paying interest not only on your balance but also on the interest you owe. Let's say you have that $1,000 balance at 15 percent—and don't buy another thing on the card. Now let's say you choose just to pay the minimum (let's say it's 2 percent of the balance), it would take you 118 months to get out of debt and you'd end up paying

$851.03 in interest for that $1,000. Yeah, you'll have paid nearly as much in interest—thanks to that compounding—as you owed in the first place.

The Dealing with Debt Plan

Regardless of whether you have high-interest debt or low-interest debt or both, you'll want to follow these next steps.

Step 1: Make a List of All of Your Debts

In the chart below, make a list of all of your debts—every credit card, mortgage, car loan, student loan, medical bill, or other loan that you have. This may take some time, as I'm asking you not only to list them, but also to find the interest rate you're paying, minimum amount owed, date payment is due, and total amount owed. This will typically be listed on the statement, and if not, you can find it online or by calling the company. Leave the column "what I'll pay each month" blank until Step 2. To do this in thirty minutes a day, break it into certain types of debts on each day (say mortgage and home equity on Day 1, credit cards on Day 2, student loans on Day 3). *Estimated time: 1 to 3 hours.*

Debt	Company name	Account Number	Interest rate	Minimum amount owed each month	Total amount owed	What I'll pay each month	Date each month payment is due
Mortgage							
Home equity loan or line of credit							
Credit card							
Credit card							
Credit card							
Car loan							
Student loan							
Other:							
Other:							

Step 2: Lower Your Debts

I'm not going to sugarcoat this: Step 2 could take a while—possibly upward of five hours if you have a number of debts. But this is time so, so well spent. Slashing your interest rates on debts can literally save you tens of thousands of dollars. The savings you get could even pay for a year or more of college! To get there, you're going to tackle one debt at a time, one hour a day, until you're finished. I'm going to make this as easy and painless as possible by walking you through it.

Lower Credit Card Interest Rates

Take a look at the chart you made in Step 1, and start with the highest-interest debt you have. This is likely a credit card. So follow these steps:

1. **Use the site NerdWallet.com to find a new, lower-interest card that will make sense for you.** They have 1,700 cards in their database and can find one that will give you a low rate. Also it may be worth looking into offers that will give you a 0 percent interest rate on balance transfers (see sidebar below). *Estimated time: 30 minutes.*

2. **See what that card will charge for a balance transfer.** A balance transfer means you move the balance of your higher interest card onto this new, lower-interest card. Use a balance transfer calculator (Bankrate.com has a great one called the Credit Card Balance Transfer Calculator; there's a link to it on my website) to see if doing a balance transfer will make financial sense for you. If you can pay the card off quickly, it may make sense to do a card that offers 0 percent introductory APR for a certain amount of time. If you can't pay it off quickly, it may make more sense just to transfer to one with a lower rate overall. *Estimated time: 30 minutes.*

Understanding the 0 Percent Balance Transfer

Let's say you have $2,000 in credit card debt on a card that charges 16 percent interest—and want to transfer to a card that has a 0 percent introductory rate for fifteen months and a balance transfer fee of 3 percent, which is pretty typical. In this case, the balance transfer itself will cost you $60 (3 percent of $2,000). If you left the debt on your current card, you'd need to pay roughly $148 a month to repay the debt in fifteen months and would end up paying more than $270 in interest. If, however, you did the balance transfer, you'd need to pay about $134 a month to repay it in fifteen months and wouldn't owe any interest. This move would end up saving you more than $200 even though you paid $60 to transfer the balance, thanks to the fact that you'd avoid the $270 in interest charges.

	Current Card (16% annual interest)	New Card (0% interest for 15 months)
Debt	$2,000	$2,000
Interest (15 months)	$270	$0
Fees	$0	$60
Total Paid	$2,270	$2,060

Of course, there's a big catch with balance transfer cards with that 0 percent interest rate: If you don't pay that balance during the 0 percent introductory period, you'll likely pay a high interest rate when that period ends. (See page 183 for how much interest can cost you.)

3. **Call your current credit card company and ask them to lower your interest rate.** This used to work better than it does now, unfortunately, but still can yield results if you are a good customer who always pays on time. Come to this call armed with other credit card offers you found on NerdWallet that are lower interest. Say something like, "I found another credit card offer of X terms and before I go with that company I wanted to see if you could match this offer." If they think you might leave them as a client, they will be more willing to negotiate. If that person can't make this happen, ask to speak to a supervisor. *Estimated time: 30 minutes.*

4. **Take the best action.** If your current card company won't lower your rate, and/or it makes financial sense to do a balance transfer, do it. But beware: If you do transfer your balance, you should know that many balance transfer cards have low intro rates (say 0 percent for six months) but those rates shoot up if your balance isn't paid by then—some as high as almost 25 percent! You can see what the rate will be after that 0 percent introductory period by reading the credit card terms. So make sure you pay it off before the deadline. I recommend putting reminders on your calendar. Also, some cards have different interest rates for the transferred balance versus new purchases; be sure you know what those are. It can, in some cases, make sense to open one card for a balance transfer at 0 percent—knowing you will definitely pay it off when the period ends—and another low-rate card for new purchases. Use the calculators on Bankrate.com to play with the numbers. *Estimated time: 30 minutes to 1½ hours.*

Refinance Your Mortgage

Refinancing your mortgage can cut your monthly payments sometimes by $100 or more, and the total amount you end up paying to the bank. (See page 38.) But, of course, like with anything financial, there are possible pitfalls: First, when you refinance, you pay closing costs, which average more than $2,000, so that cost must be factored in. And, when you refinance, if you extend the term of your loan (say, you had twenty years left on your original loan and when you refinance you do so for a thirty-year loan) that could mean you pay more interest over the life of the loan, which may not make it financially worth it after all. Still, this can make financial sense, so here's what it takes to find that out and refinance if it makes sense for you.

1. **Find out what interest rate you currently pay on your mortgage.** This should appear on your monthly statement or you can get by calling your lender. *Estimated time: 15 minutes.*

Fixed Rate vs. Adjustable Rate Mortgages

With a fixed rate mortgage, your interest rate is decided upon at the start of the mortgage and it never changes. With an adjustable rate mortgage, the rate does change. Typically, the initial interest rate on an adjustable rate mortgage is lower than with a fixed rate mortgage but then, after some set period of time—for example, three, five, or ten years—it rises (and in some loans falls), usually as interest rates in the economy rise/fall (the terms of this are laid out in the loan). These kinds of loans can make sense for people who only plan to stay in their home a short time. Bankrate.com has great resources for comparing the pros and cons of each of these types of loans.

---

2. **Check out Bankrate.com for the going rate on mortgages in your area now.** Are rates lower than what you're paying? If so, it may be time to refinance. Zillow.com has a simple-to-use refinance calculator. You put in your current rate, expected new rate, and expected refinancing fees (typically about 3 to

6 percent of the total mortgage loan), to see if this makes sense for you. *Estimated time: 15 minutes.*

3. **Find a loan with better terms.** This is where you'll have to do some work. A good place to start is Bankrate.com, which has both trustworthy how-to guides and mortgage rates posted from a variety of lenders. You'll want to call each lender and discuss the terms you can get, making sure to ask about the new rates, refinancing costs, and more. Just beware of extending the term of your loan, as this will mean you pay more interest over the life of the loan. *Estimated time: 30 minutes per call.*

4. **Consider using a mortgage broker.** If you find you should refinance but are super busy, a mortgage broker can find you competitive refinancing offers. He or she gets paid when you close, typically 1 percent of the loan amount, which can be a lot. But the time and effort to compare lenders, fill out the paperwork, et cetera, sometimes make this worth it. *Estimated time: The paperwork and logistics for a refinance can take upward of 4 hours, though you can do this in short chunks of time to break it up.*

Refinance Your Student Loans

By now, you've probably consolidated your federal student loans and feel like there isn't much more to do but pay down those debts. But refinancing those loans could get a lower interest rate. Yes, even federal student loans—those loans you got from the government—can be refinanced, and it can save you a lot of money! One study found that it saves $14,000 on average. This is thanks to a load of new companies—like SoFi and Earnest—that now do this. SoFi, for example, doesn't have any brick-and-mortar locations so it can keep costs down, and unlike traditional lenders, it looks at factors beyond just your credit score, including education and career, when making loan decisions. The big risk here is you lose the generous repayment perks that come with federal student loans, like the ability to set up payment options based on your income if you aren't making much. But if you're nearly positive you'll never need those anyway and you can get a much lower rate if you refinance, refinancing can be a good option. I like the site StudentLoanHero.com for helpful calculators and advice on whether this might be a smart idea for you. *Estimated time: Like with mortgage refinancing, the paperwork and logistics for a refinance can take hours—and you should read the fine print—though you can do this in short chunks of time to break it up.*

Refinance Your Car Loan

This process is surprisingly easy because no appraisal is required and fees are minimal. So if you paid too much when you financed your car, or if your credit score has improved, this is something to consider. Just be aware that many lenders want a car to be less than five years old and worth at least $7,500 before they will refinance your loan. Bankrate.com is your go-to site here. It lists auto loan rates on its site so you can compare, and has resources on lenders who will refinance your car loan and helpful articles about how to do it.

Estimated time: This, too, can take hours, especially considering it's smart to read the fine print, but take your time and do it!

Negotiate Your Medical Bills and Get on a Repayment Plan

If you're facing a high medical bill, it is worth it to negotiate that down. Here's how:

1. **Ask the hospital for an itemized statement.** When you get it look for errors on the bill like things you were charged for but didn't receive (these are insanely common) and things that the insurance company should have covered but didn't.

You will likely need your policy's explanation of benefits to compare. Your insurance company can send this to you, if they haven't already, just call and ask. *Estimated time: 1 to 2 hours, though if you had multiple doctors and procedures, this could take significantly longer.*

2. **Know what a fair price for your procedure should have been.** HealthcareBluebook.com is a decent place to start for this. *Estimated time: 30 minutes.*

3. **Call the hospital.** Armed with the information you found, try to negotiate your total bill down. Hospitals are used to patients defaulting on bills so they are one of the more willing debtors to negotiate. Once you've negotiated, if you can't afford to pay the bill in full, ask for a repayment plan. *Estimated time: 30 minutes to 1 hour.*

If this all sounds too complicated, there are experts and sites that, for a fee, will help you. You can find a medical billing advocate who will go through your bills for you and help you save through the National Association of Healthcare Advocacy Consultants website. Some charge by the hour, while others charge as a percentage of savings, which works in your favor because you only pay if they save you money.

Step 3: Figure Out How Much to Pay on Each Debt

Good news! You've now done the hard part, so this step shouldn't take you more than a couple hours. Yay! Your strategy for paying these debts off is simple. Each month, pay as much as you can on the debt with the highest interest rate, and pay the minimum payment on all others. It may take a little thought to figure out how much more than the minimum you can pay on your highest-interest debt, but by now, you have likely cut a lot off your spending.

Here's a list of online calculators to help you figure out how quickly you might be able to pay off those debts:

* Credit card debt: Bankrate.com's Credit Card Calculator
* Student loan debt: StudentLoanHero.com and Bankrate.com
* Other debt payoff goals: Bankrate.com
* Retirement savings: AARP.org

Remember that all of these calculators, and others mentioned in the book, are also available on my website, CateyHill.com.

To get an idea of what paying off that debt might look like, here's a chart showing approximately how much you need to pay by week and by month to pay off a credit card debt in three years.

	12% Interest Rate		15% Interest Rate	
Total Debt	Your Weekly Payment	Your Monthly Payment	Your Weekly Payment	Your Monthly Payment
$5,000	$38	$166	$40	$173
$8,000	$61	$266	$64	$277
$11,000	$84	$365	$88	$381
$14,000	$107	$465	$112	$485

Eradicate Credit Card Debt in 3 Years

Once the highest interest item is paid off, repeat this with the second highest interest loan. You will continue this until all debts are paid off. Yes, this may take years, but it's simple to do—and effective.

The Minimal Math Debt Repayment Strategy

If you want to pay off your debt without having to do a lot of calculations, here's the quick method:

1. For the first month, pay at least $50 to $100 more than the minimum (or more than you're paying currently) off the highest interest debt, and pay the minimum due on all other debts.
2. Keep upping this amount each month until you can't anymore.
3. Continue paying that maximum amount that you can afford every month until the debt is paid off.
4. Start paying off your debt with the next highest interest rate using the amount from Step 3 until it's gone. And so on. You'll pay that debt off faster than you think.

When NOT to Hurry to Pay Off Debts

If you've got a low-interest debt (below about 4 to 5 percent), in many cases, there isn't a big hurry to pay if off quickly. Instead, pay the minimums on that debt and contribute more to your retirement fund. (Unless you're already super on track with retirement savings, in which case tackle those debts!) The reasoning is simple: Over the long term, you'll likely earn more than 5 percent on your retirement fund each year, and that debt is costing you less than that.

The Lifestyle Debt Repayment Strategy

If you're having difficulty finding the extra money to pay off your debt, try making a simple plan. Write down your goal for when you want to have the debt paid off. Then figure out, using one of the calculators listed above, how much you need to save each week. Finally, figure out specific things you can do to set that money aside.

Here's an example of what that might look like. Let's say I owe $1,000 on my credit card, which has a 14 percent interest rate. I make a New Year's resolution to pay it off in a year. First, I use the Bankrate.com calculator to figure out the weekly amount. It tells me I need to save $88.79 each month to pay off my debt in a year. So I did $88.79 × 12 months in a year to get the annual cost of $1,065; then divided that by 52 weeks to get the weekly cost of $20.49. Know you just have to figure out something you can do differently to set that money aside. Here's an example:

Goal

Pay off my $1,000 MasterCard bill (14 percent interest rate)

When I Want to Achieve This Goal

1 year from now

How Much I Need to Save Each Week

$20.49

My Plan to Save Each Week

1. Four days per week—Monday through Thursday—I will pack a lunch for work instead of going out to lunch (savings of a little over $5 per day or $20 per week). And I'll alternate weeks with my husband, so we can switch off on the burden.
2. I will grocery shop on Sunday afternoon to get the low-cost ingredients to make lunches for the week.
3. I will schedule time in my calendar both for the shopping trip and in the evenings Sunday through Wednesday to make my lunch.

Chapter 14

Getting the Right Insurance (and Other Ways to Protect Your Family)

As a mom, you'll do anything to protect your kids—and yet plenty of moms don't have some of the most important things they need to protect them: all the right kinds of insurance. You need insurance. Period. It's what protects you and your family from accidents, lawsuits, natural disasters, bad health, and more. This chapter will walk you through what types of insurance you need and how to get it if you don't have it. Plus, we'll talk about the onetime things you need to protect your family, like a will, power of attorney, and more.

The Money-Savvy Mama's Quick Guide

The 5 things you need to do to get your finances on track.

- Manage your basic living costs
- Smartly pay down your debt
- **Get the right insurance**
- Build up emergency savings
- Save for periods of financial freedom (and eventual retirement)

You need five main types of insurance:

1. Health (see Chapter 8)
2. Homeowner's/renter's (see Chapter 3)
3. Auto (see Chapter 6)
4. Disability
5. Life

We looked at the first three already, in Part I, but we haven't yet talked about how much life and disability insurance you have, so that's what I'll do here.

Disability Insurance 101

What is it? Disability insurance provides you with income in the event that you can't work due to injury or illness; typically it will replace about 60 percent of your income. There are two types of disability insurance: short-term and long-term. **Short-term disability insurance** pays you some income for a short period of time, usually six weeks to two years. **Long-term disability** insurance typically picks up where short-term disability leaves off, paying income for years, usually until you can work again or up until your full retirement age, which is when many people begin claiming Social Security. Often your employer gives you this benefit, so call HR and ask if they do and how much of your salary the disability insurance will replace. Women who have short-term disability insurance often use this benefit to provide them some income if they take time off to have a child.

Who needs it? If you (and/or your spouse) have a job, and your family would suffer without your income, it's a good idea to get it.

How much does it cost? If you don't get it from your employer, it won't be cheap. Long-term disability insurance, for example, will cost you about 1 to 4 percent of your annual salary each year.

Sound like way too much? Here are a few ways to save:

1. **Opt for a longer elimination period.** The elimination period is the amount of time you have to wait before the insurance company will start paying you income. So you might change this period from 90 days to 180 days. Just make sure you have some way to pay your bills during this time.

2. **Buy the policy at the same time as another person or a few other people.** The company might give you a discount for doing so. Buying with a man (your spouse even, if this applies) can be a big money-saver, too, because men often qualify for lower rates—sometimes 30 percent or more off the rates you might get alone—thanks to the fact that they're considered lower risk. It's worth finding out.

3. **Remember, something is better than nothing.** Even if you can't afford all the coverage you think you need, getting some income each month if you become disabled is better than getting none.

How much do I need and where do I get it? Use the calculator on Life Happens.org to figure out how much your family needs. The amount your employer provides (if they do provide it) may not be enough, so check to see if they offer you the option to purchase more. It's important that you get a policy that is both noncancelable (the company can't just drop you) and guaranteed renewable (meaning you can renew the policy as long as you want). LifeHappens.org can also help you find an agent to shop for a policy for you, and has other helpful resources.

Life Insurance

If you have kids, you likely need life insurance, as it provides them with money if you die. (I know, not something anyone wants to think about!) Get a guaranteed renewable policy. For most people, term life insurance is the right choice. **Term life insurance** pays your spouse and kids enough money for ten, twenty, or thirty years. You pick the term based on how long you think your family will need it. You want enough life insurance so that your family could live comfortably up until an age when they could support themselves. Use the calculator at LifeHappens.org to help you figure this out. Often your employer will offer you life insurance, but make sure this is enough. You can shop on your own as well. NerdWallet .com has a section that lets you compare current quotes from different insurers.

Other Important Ways to Protect Your Family from Harm

Most parents know they need a will, but also think—eh, nothing will happen to me, and if it does, my sister (or whoever) will take over. I've literally seen firsthand how untrue that all is: My husband is an estate-planning lawyer, and he often deals with situations in which parents didn't have wills and other necessary documents and then passed away. (Our dinner conversations aren't always that uplifting.) Let me tell you: What happens when parents don't have a will is horrendous and puts a huge burden on families. And the hardest part is knowing that to prevent all of this, they could have met with a local lawyer for literally an hour or two. Instead, the kids are put through hell and the family's estate has to pay thousands in fees. So here's what I'll tell you: Wouldn't you rather face up to the reality that you could pass away or become incapacitated—however unlikely it may be—than make your kids go through that? What you need to do to prevent that is simple: Just get these documents, store them away, and don't think of them again for a while. You'll have the peace of mind that your family is protected, but probably won't have to worry about any of this for decades!

1. **The will:** It states who you want to take care of your children in the long term, as well as how you want the things you own to be passed down to your kids and others. It's great, but it has limitations: It only goes into effect if you die, so if you are merely incapacitated (say you are injured and can't make decisions for yourself) it won't go into effect. So you need a short-term plan in place, too—see #3 below.

2. Every parent that has a child under age eighteen should include in their will a trust for their children. If something happens to both parents, any money that would be for the benefit of the kids goes into that trust fund. If you didn't have this trust in your will, any money going to your children would be restricted by the court and anytime the person taking care of your kids needed money—for anything from school books to clothing—they would have to go to the court and get permission to get the money.

3. **Power of attorney:** This allows another person to act on your behalf in legal matters if you can't. Most people are shocked to learn that their spouse can't make financial decisions for them without a power of attorney. So, let's say you become incapacitated and can't pay your bills; this document would allow that person to have access to your banking and

other financial accounts and do that for you. If you don't have this document, your spouse or family will have to go into court to get access to your money, which can be very expensive.

4. **Health care proxy/health care power of attorney:** This allows you to appoint someone you trust to make health care decisions for you if you can't do it yourself. You care because if you lose the ability to make decisions for yourself (say you were in a horrible car accident and are hooked up to life support), this allows someone you trust and choose to make them for you. Once you appoint this person, you will want to discuss this with the person.

5. **A living will:** With a living will, you work with a lawyer to specify your health care wishes should you become incapacitated, rather than appointing someone to do it. Some estate-planning attorneys prefer this to a health care proxy/health care power of attorney because then the person herself decides about her care; many others do not. The issue with a living will is that medical issues can be complicated, and there is no way for you to cover everything that could happen to you in a living will. Any ambiguity could be misinterpreted by the hospital, which could mean you don't get the results you wanted.

While the online legal services might have been okay before you had kids and didn't have many assets, it's probably a good idea now to hire a professional to draw up these documents for you. Once kids get involved, you want a professional looking over everything! The whole meeting shouldn't take more than an hour or two. Typically a lawyer will charge you a flat fee to draw up a will and those other documents listed above—anything from about $500 to $2,000 is what you'll pay (this will vary depending on where you live). Ideally look for a lawyer that specializes in both estate planning and elder- and special-needs planning. If you don't have a personal referral for a lawyer, call your local county bar association; they will probably have a referral service.

Chapter 15

Building Up Your Emergency Savings

I know you've probably picked up your share of personal finance books, tried to read them, gotten to the savings and investing part, and then dropped them in terror because there were SO, SO MANY things you "had" to know to deal with your financial situation. I mean, seriously, some of those books weigh more than a newborn baby! And while they have great advice, I know far too many moms who have taken one look at those weighty tomes and thought *That would make a nice doorstopper* and never picked them up again. Frankly, who has the time to get through a finance manifesto with a screaming baby/rambunctious toddler/pouty preteen needing their constant attention?

But remember, everything you need to do to be a financially savvy mama can fit on a Post-it note. And understanding and doing a decent job with your savings is way easier than it looks! I promise, it will be fast and relatively painless. Then you're on to the part where we talk about spending that gravy money!

The Money-Savvy Mama's Quick Guide

The 5 things you need to do to get your finances on track.

- Manage your basic living costs
- Smartly pay down your debt
- Get the right insurance
- **Build up emergency savings**
- Save for periods of financial freedom (and eventual retirement)

So let's dive into emergency savings. As anyone of us who lived through the recession knows, job losses can and do happen—sometimes when you're least expecting it. Plus, in a given year, nearly half of Americans are hit with a significant expense they didn't expect, like car trouble or a trip to the ER, according to American Express data. And it's often something that surprises the crap out of you! My most recent one: My husband went out to our car one chilly morning and it wouldn't start; we took it into the shop and they told us some kind of rodent had eaten through the wiring. Disgusting! Apparently this is a thing in the city because rodents climb into the hoods of cars to stay warm. The bill was absurdly expensive (of course!).

Whether it's a job loss or a medical bill, a car repair or a roof repair, one thing is true: Life's surprises can be pricey. And it's for the surprising things in life, which happen to the best of us, that you need a pile of savings that you use in case of emergency. Having this emergency fund will also give you more peace of mind, because when—not if—the unexpected happens, you won't have to worry as much about how you're going to pay for that and everything else. Just be sure to replenish your fund each time you dive into it.

In an ideal world, you would have enough saved to pay your living expenses for nine to twelve months or more. That emergency fund could be used if you or your partner lost a job or couldn't work for a long period, which is often people's worst-case scenario, or for something more minor, but still an emergency, like a car repair. I know that amount (nine to twelve months of expenses!!) seems crazy impossible, but don't get overwhelmed: Start small. Think about putting at least three months of living expenses into savings for now. One easy way to begin is to use the savings-goal feature on money management and budgeting site Mint.com, but you don't need a fancy app.

Remember, if you're still paying down credit card debt, concentrate on that first, as well as putting up to what your employer matches in your 401(k). Once you get that credit card debt erased, you can up your retirement savings and start building up an emergency fund, using all the money you used to be paying the credit card company in interest.

To keep yourself on track, you might want to make yourself a goal worksheet that lays out your personal savings plan that look something like this:

Goal

Save $18,000 into my emergency savings fund, so that I'd have $2,000 per month to live on for 9 months if I lost my job.

When I Want to Achieve This Goal

2 years

How Much I Need to Save Each Week

$173 per week

My Plan to Save Each Week

- Cancel family gym membership; work out at home instead. $30 per week saved

- Cancel cable, have kids stream via Hulu and Netflix instead. $20 per week saved
- Slash the family new clothes/accessories budget: $10 per week saved
- Find a cheaper cell phone plan: $10 per week saved
- Stop buying beverages like juice and seltzer at the grocery; stick to your tap water (assuming it's safe): $10 per week saved
- Eat out as a family every other week instead of once a week: $20 per week saved
- Have you and your spouse pack lunch for at least three days a work week: $30 per week saved
- Have you and your spouse shun Starbucks at least three days a work week: $10 per week saved
- Go vegetarian two days a week: $10 per week saved
- Let your once-a-month cleaning service go; have the kids take over her duties slowly throughout the month: $25 per week saved

To figure out that I'd need to save $173 each week, I simply divided $18,000 by 104, which is the number of weeks in two years. Admittedly you may be earning some interest on this money (though at the writing of this book savings account interest rates were paltry). But for the sake of simplicity—and because it doesn't hurt usually to save a bit more—I didn't include interest in these calculations.

Still, you want to put the money you're saving somewhere safe, where the money is pretty easy to withdraw and earning interest. A high-interest savings account works, as would a money market account, which is a type of savings account that usually earns a little higher interest rate than standard savings accounts. Bankrate.com lists savings accounts and money market accounts with higher than average interest rates. Open one and start saving in there (as long as you're not still paying down high-interest debt).

Be sure to explain to the kids, if they are old enough to understand, why you are making these cuts; these kinds of conversations about money will help your kids for many years to come.

The "Build a Wall" Trick to Saving Money

One of the reasons we spend so much is because it's easier than ever to spend. Gorgeous new throw pillows to freshen up your living room are a click away, a relaxing beach vacay (at a discount!) can be had with just a few swipes, the amazing sale Overstock is having lands in your inbox at least once a week. That ease with which we can spend is a HUGE problem, though. About one-fifth of our spending—and in many cases more—is related to things we absolutely, positively DO NOT NEED. So, I'm going to give you a simple piece of advice that will likely save you at least $100 to $500 this year if you do it: Build a wall.

What I mean is this: You have to build a wall between you and buying things. Make it harder to buy. And doing this, is simple:

* **Unsubscribe from store email lists.**
* I know, you love them, but those "sales" that land in your inbox usually do more to get you to buy things you don't need than they do to get you a deal on something you do. The sales, of course, are only for a "limited time" (or so the store pretends) and that taps right into our evolutionary history. Humans are primed to horde when things are scarce, so a limited-time sale tempts you to buy! You think, *But I'll never*

get this price again! But you likely will get that price again. I researched how fake listing prices were for MarketWatch back in 2014. Here's an excerpt from that story:

> Many of the stores that offer the most frequent coupons and discounts also tailor the asking prices of items so that even coupons and sales don't mean real savings. For example, as of July 11 [2014], frequent discounter J.C. Penney advertises that the "original price" of its Ninja NJ600 Blender is $145.00 and that it's now on sale for $99.00. Meanwhile, at Target, Bed Bath & Beyond, and Best Buy, that blender is listed at and selling for $99.99 and at Amazon, it's listed at $109.99 and selling for $96.35.

* If you MUST get these emails, at least have them sent to a separate email address and then check it just once a week or less.
* **Don't save your credit card information on any site.**
* If you have to get up, find your credit card, and enter in that information, this will give you what I call an "automatic question period" in which you will wonder—wait, is this really worth it? If the information is just stored in the site, a few clicks later, you've bought the item without thinking about it.
* **Always check out as a guest.**
* Even better than not saving card information is to always check out as a guest. Then when you buy from that store again, you will have to enter all of your information into the site.
* **Delete spending apps from your phone.**
* Do you really need Amazon or Target—or other apps that allow you to shop—right on your phone? Delete them and

it will force you, if you want to shop there, to do it on your
desktop.

* **Turn off push notifications.**
* If you allow certain stores to send you push notifications, stop
  it: You are essentially just letting them infiltrate your wallet.
  You probably weren't thinking about shopping at that store
  and then "bam" push notification, and there you go.
* **Follow these two "old school" rules.**
* You've likely heard both these rules before but I think they're
  so good they bear repeating:
  o **Practice the seventy-two-hour rule:** Before you buy
    something that's over say $50, make yourself wait three
    days. When the seventy-two-hour window is up, revisit
    the item; if it's still a must-have go ahead and get it. But
    I find that most of the time, it's not. Budget expert Liz
    Frugalwoods once told me that during this window she
    thinks about her long-term goals, these would be anything
    from getting to take your next vacation to going to work
    part-time instead of full-time. "When you pit a sweater
    against living the life of your dreams, it's easy not to buy
    the sweater," she told me.
  o **Use cash:** If you're overspending, you can turn that around
    by using cash. People who use credit cards spend roughly
    12 to 18 percent more than those who use cash, according
    to a study by Dun & Bradstreet.
* **Beware of social media.**
* Okay, I know you aren't going to delete your Facebook
  account but I want to make you aware of this phenomenon,
  so you can avoid this trap. Nearly four in ten adults with a
  social media account say seeing another person's post about
  what they recently bought or a vacation they recently went on
  spurred them to look into a similar purchase, according to

data from the American Institute of Certified Public Accountants. It's a new definition of "comparison shopping" and you can obviously see how it can spur unnecessary spending. Just remember: People only post the "best" version of themselves online; I can pretty much guarantee you that it wasn't those Jimmy Choos that made your friend look so happy in subsequent photos.

Chapter 16

Saving for Periods of Financial Freedom (and Eventual Retirement)

Okay, I know I am in the minority with this opinion, but I think this idea of "retirement"—the notion that at sixty-five-ish you just quit your job entirely and sit on the beach all day, after working full-speed ahead on the career path every year before that—is kind of dead for many people. Survey after survey shows that most people (three in four typically) expect to work past sixty-five. They don't expect, of course, to keep going at 100 percent in an office job, but they hope to do something like work part-time on a passion project or for a nonprofit they care about. My latest thing is working at an animal rescue place! And, many of us would like to switch careers to something we love *before* sixty-five, even if it doesn't pay as well. You may want to work only part-time while the kids are young or right before they go to college, then go back to full-time when they go to school. This, admittedly, is not easy, so it's a factor to consider when planning your savings if you think you might want to do something like this before you turn sixty-five.

The Money-Savvy Mama's Quick Guide

The 5 things you need to do to get your finances on track.

- Manage your basic living costs
- Smartly pay down your debt
- Get the right insurance
- Build up emergency savings
- **Save for periods of financial freedom (and eventual retirement)**

That's why I'm calling this section "saving for financial freedom." Ideally, you'll try to sock away 13 to 15 percent of your salary each month into your 401(k) for eventual retirement. Typically your employer lets you select the percentage of your income you want to contribute so this rule makes it super easy for you to do. Then you'll put more into a savings or brokerage account, so you can save for other periods of financial freedom, in which you might, say, switch careers or become a stay-at-home mom for a while. We'll talk about this more in the following section.

Another rule for saving for retirement, according to Fidelity:

By age 30, you should have your current before-tax salary saved for retirement.

By 40, you should have three times your salary saved.

By 50, six times your salary saved.

By 60, eight times your salary saved.

By 67, (retirement age) ten times your salary saved.

(See sidebar on page 214 to see how easy saving is thanks to the power of compound interest.) If you want a more specific estimate on what you personally should be saving for retirement, check out the calculators on Bankrate.com.

Retirement Savings If You Have High-Interest Debt

If you're in high-interest debt (anything with an interest rate over about 6 to 7 percent) like credit card debt, you should contribute up to the amount your employer will match into your 401(k) because that's literally free money, but anything beyond that should be put toward paying off that high interest debt quickly. Once you've gotten rid of the debt, focus on saving more for retirement.

If You Want to Downshift or Change Careers Before Retirement

If you plan to keep working past sixty-five but don't plan on having a traditional career path (i.e., work full-time without switching careers until you hit retirement), I think it is worth exploring how you might want to save a little differently. Yes, you still MUST contribute to your retirement account, but if you have other goals (a few years of part-time work, for example), you may need to shift your savings a bit. And because all of your "financial freedom" goals will be different, I think it is absolutely worth meeting with a financial planner to discuss how this might happen for you. You want to be able to save for retirement so you can eventually stop working (sometimes we have to stop, even if we don't want to) and be able to have periods during your career where you can downshift a bit, if needed. Because you are penalized 10 percent if you withdraw from your 401(k) before age fifty-nine and a half, it may not make sense for you to put every extra dime into your 401(k).

The average family can save enough for retirement by socking away just $300 per month.

Let's say you're thirty years old today, and your family makes $50,000 a year. You'll want to aim to have about ten times your income (or $500,000) saved for retirement when you hit sixty-seven. That sounds super scary, right? But it's easier to do than you might think.

Over the next thirty-seven years, save $300 each month for retirement—turn to page 224 to see where you'll come up with this extra $300—and you'll hit your target, assuming you earn 6 percent each year, on average, on your money (P.S. That 6 percent is TOTALLY doable over the long-haul!).

Help! I Don't Really Know What a 401(k) or IRA Are

Don't be embarrassed! These things are complicated, but here's what you need to know. Both a 401(k) and an IRA are basically special financial accounts where you keep money for retirement. Some people, like public school teachers or those who work for a nonprofit, might have a 403(b), which is their version of a 401(k).

The deal is that you get a tax break on the money you put in these accounts as long as you keep it in the account and don't spend it before you turn fifty-nine and a half. But rather than just leave this money sitting there for decades as if you put cash in a shoebox under the bed, it's invested so it can earn interest. (Don't panic, we'll get to easy ways to invest later in this book.)

With a 401(k) or 403(b), you tell your employer what percentage of your income you want to save in the account; they automatically deduct this from your paycheck. They make these deductions from your pretax salary. This means that if you make $50,000 per year, and contribute $5,000 to your 401(k), when you pay your taxes in April, you will only be taxed as if you made $45,000 a year—that's $50,000 minus the $5,000 you put into your 401(k). Meanwhile, your $5,000 is earning even more money from being invested. And many employers match part of what you contribute, which means you're actually getting far more than the $5,000 you put in. You also defer paying taxes on your earnings until you withdraw the money in retirement. Because most people have a lower income when they're retired, this means they're in a lower tax bracket than they were when they put the money in.

An IRA works nearly the same as a 401(k) does, but it is not set up by your employer; instead, you call a bank and have one set up for yourself. You might do this if your employer doesn't offer a 401(k) or if you change jobs, and don't want to or can't roll over what is in your old 401(k) to your new employer's 401(k). There is also something called a Roth IRA, which you also set up yourself, but in a Roth IRA you contribute money that you've already paid taxes on. Then, when you take the money out in retirement, you will not have to pay any taxes on it. Though pretty rare, some employers offer a Roth 401(k), which is a 401(k) in which you contribute after-tax money.

The Easy Way to Set Up Your 401(k)

Typically, you can enroll in your employer's 401(k) plan—or 403(b) plan if you work for a public school, charity, or religious organization—either when you start a new job or during open enrollment, which is usually around November for the following year. Most employers will email you to let you know when open enrollment starts or you can call HR and ask. It's easy to sign up for it—seriously this usually takes maybe fifteen minutes. The harder part is picking your investments, but I'm going to walk you through an easy way to do that. For now, you just need to know that you'll want to give yourself a good three hours or more to research your investment options. Usually, open enrollment lasts at least a few weeks so you can pick a week and look into your investment options for thirty minutes each evening until you find ones that suit you. You will also be able to switch investments in the future so you're not permanently stuck with your choices.

A decent plan will have a variety of low-cost funds to choose from, including major stock index funds like the S&P 500 and bond funds including U.S. Treasuries (see page 220).

If you don't have a decent 401(k) from your employer, it's a good idea to at least have some type of retirement fund. So if your plan is lackluster, call Vanguard (they're my pick because they offer a lot of low-cost investment options) and ask to open an IRA. Just like with a 401(k), the opening of the account won't take long, it's the picking of investments that's the hard part. Not sure if your 401(k) is decent or not? See page 223 for a quick guide to help you tell.

Once you enroll in the plan and pick your investments, you set it and forget it. Seriously, don't mess with it again until next year. You may see headlines about how the stock market is down but even then, leave your investments alone! Study after study shows that people who tinker with their investments too often tend to get worse returns than those that don't.

I Just Don't Have the Time/Desire/Energy to Deal with This Investing Thing

Don't worry, you're not alone. I wouldn't be writing this section otherwise! What you're about to read next isn't the advice you're going to hear in a lot of books, which give you a step-by-step guide on investing in your retirement fund. I've been writing about personal finance for a decade now, and I have learned this: Even after reading (okay skimming through) a book about this stuff, most people still don't feel confident in their ability to pick investments. You absolutely can do it yourself—and I am going to show you how—but if you still don't feel confident, or just don't want to deal, it may be worth it to hire a pro and let them advise you on picking investments. But you'll just want to know enough to check the pro's work, so stick with me just a little longer.

If you're wealthy, you'll have no problem finding a financial adviser. They'll look at your fat six-figure portfolio, charge you a fee to manage it (usually some percentage of the total assets in there) and boom, you're in business. But many people don't have enough money for those kinds of advisers to manage. That used to be a HUGE problem for regular folks, but not anymore. There are now a number of fee-only advisers who charge by the hour. You want a fee-only adviser, as they don't make commissions for selling you certain kinds of investments that might not be good for you. For a busy parent, it can be smart, at least every couple years during open enrollment time, to hire an hourly fee-only adviser to help you pick the right investments and ensure that you're on track financially.

Where Regular, Middle-Class Families Can Find Financial Help

If you want help from a real person:

- **Garrett Planning Network:** This site lists hundreds of vetted, fee-only advisers, with no minimum account requirements (meaning that even if your retirement funds are modest, they will still work with you) and no long-term commitments to an adviser. You typically pay these advisers by the hour, $150 to $300 an hour is common. You can put a cap on the amount of time they devote to you (nicely explain that you're on a budget). Ask them what they need in advance and have all of the information they need ready to go. It shouldn't take them long to check your current investments and tell you where to tweak them. It's okay if there isn't an adviser in your town; an adviser can work for you remotely by phone.

- **Vanguard Personal Adviser Services:** I like Vanguard because their investment options are usually solid and low cost, and now the company has a feature that allows you to work with one of its advisers. The cost is about 0.3 percent of your portfolio and you must have a minimum of $50,000. You can roll old 401(k)s into a Vanguard account to make this work.

- **Personal Capital:** Personal Capital has a free site to help you budget and save money (much like budgeting site Mint). You link all of your financial accounts to the secure site. If you have $25,000 or more, you can pay a fee (typically .89 percent of your total portfolio or less, which means you'd pay $890 to them if you had $100,000 in the account) for access to a financial adviser. The adviser can help you pick 401(k) investments.

If you don't mind automated/computer help:

- There are a ton of so-called robo-adviser sites, where you link your accounts, and the computer can tell you if your retirement investments seem solid. Here are some of the best:

- **Betterment:** For a fee of between 0.25 to 0.40 percent per year of your total account, the site will tell you if you're paying too much in fees, if you're invested in the right things for your age, et cetera. No minimum account balance.

- **Wealthfront:** This one works similarly to Betterment but has a $500 minimum and charges an annual fee of 0.25 percent of your portfolio.

How to Vet a Financial Adviser

There are a number of great online resources to help make sure your financial adviser is solid. Consumer Reports has a great guide, as does Kiplinger. In a nutshell, you want to know:

1. **If he's done anything shady in the past.** Use BrokerCheck (it's free, go to brokercheck.finra.org) to look him and the firm up.
2. **Does he act as a fiduciary?** Ask him this—fiduciaries are required to act in your best interest and to tell you exactly how they make money.
3. **How is the adviser paid?** Look for a fee-only adviser. An adviser who is paid a flat fee or a percentage of your total portfolio is much less likely to push investments that don't make sense for you.
4. **What are her credentials?** Those who have designations like certified financial planner (CFP) or chartered financial consultant (ChFC) have had to take extensive coursework and pass national exams. If you see someone with other credentials, look those up—they may have simply paid for them, rather than done real work and passed a test to get them.
5. **What is his experience?** Ask how long he has done this job, how many clients he has, and whether he deals with you personally or will outsource you to an associate.
6. **Get at least three references.** Call all of them.

For a list of other questions, download the financial adviser questionnaire on NAPFA.org.

What You Need to Know About Investing—Even if You're Having an Adviser Help You

I'm not going to sit here and tell you this section is going to be riveting (frankly, the ins and outs of investing are only fascinating for a small group of peeps). I'm just going to make this fast and to the point. Understand it, know it, move on.

Lingo 101:

* **Stock:** A share of ownership in a company; when you own stock, you are a shareholder who owns part of that company. Stocks are usually categorized by three things:
   a. The sector—like health care or technology—that the company falls into
   b. The type of stock, which is either "growth stock" that investors think will grow faster than average, or "value stock" that investors think are undervalued at the moment
   c. The company size: small-cap for small companies, mid-cap for midsize, and large-cap for large companies (typically large companies are less risky than small ones).
* **Bond:** This is basically an IOU. You give a company or corporation money for the bond, and they promise to pay you back on a schedule, with interest. U.S. Treasury bonds (which are issued by the federal government) are considered among the safest, while junk bonds and unrated bonds are the riskiest. Standard & Poor's and Moody's both rate bonds (with AAA or Aaa with least risk, AA or Aa the second least and on down to BBB or Bbb, which has the highest risk).
* **Mutual funds:** A mutual fund is basically just a collection of different stocks, bonds, or other investments. The good thing

about mutual funds is that they give you instant diversification, meaning that they allow you to invest in a variety of different things in one place. That's great because you don't want all your eggs in one basket. There are two different kinds of funds:

a. **Actively managed fund**—A professional chooses where to invest the money, actively buying and selling investments and deducting a fee for the work. These funds are typically more expensive for consumers than index funds below because the fees for the manager and her team's work are typically pricier than fees that come with an index fund.

b. **Index fund**—the fund simply follows a certain generally recognized list. For example, there are index funds for the S&P 500, which is a collection of five hundred different stocks of mostly large and established companies. If one company is replaced by another on this list, the index fund automatically sells the stock in the old company and buys stock in the new company—there's not a professional behind the wheel. That sounds scary but the reality is that index funds, over the long haul, tend to vastly outperform actively managed funds and charge a much lower fee, so these are things you want in your portfolio.

How to Pick Your Retirement Account Investments

So now that you know the lingo, how do you know what to put in your portfolio? Here are the four key things to focus on:

1. **Get the percentages right.** You want a nice mix of stocks (ideally index funds) and bonds. A rough rule of thumb is

this: Subtract your age from 110 or 120; that number is the percentage of your portfolio that should be in stocks. So let's say you're 30, that means that you'd want between 80 and 90 percent of the money you have invested for retirement in stocks/index funds.

2. **Diversify.** You want to have myriad different investments in your portfolio; so if one goes south, it doesn't totally sink you. Look for index funds that track the entire market, as these offer instant diversification. Usually they say so in the name (something like Total Market Index Fund or Extended Market Index Funds). Some examples are Vanguard Total Stock Market Index Fund and Fidelity Spartan Total Market Index Fund. They also have bond funds that do this like the Vanguard Total Bond Market Index Fund and the T-Rowe Price U.S. Bond Index.

3. You also want to make sure you have some international index funds, which are index funds that invest in international stocks. Usually you want about 15 to 30 percent of your total stock portfolio to be international and the remaining 70 to 85 percent in domestic/U.S.-based funds. You might see names like: Vanguard Total International Stock Index Fund and Vanguard Total Stock Market Index Fund, to indicate this.

4. **Expense ratio.** An expense ratio is the annual fee a fund charges to cover its costs. You can find out what this ratio is by looking at the prospectus of the funds you're investing in online. The lower this is the less you're paying. An index fund might charge just 0.18 percent, an actively managed fund tends to charge much more (perhaps 0.78 percent), which can add up to thousands of dollars in extra fees for you. Look for low fees!

How Do I Find Out More About a Fund?

Want a simple way to look up how good your fund is? Well, there is no perfect way, but I like Morningstar for this. First google the name of your fund and get its ticker symbol. (For example, the Vanguard Total Stock Market Index Fund has the symbol VTSMX.) Then pop that ticker into the search box on Morningstar. It will instantly show you a snapshot of the fund you're looking up. At the top of the page, next to the fund name and ticker symbol is a star rating ranging from five stars for the top 10 percent, to one star for the bottom 10 percent. You'll also find other information, like the top stocks and sectors in the fund; how much of it is U.S. versus international investments; and the mix of bonds, stocks, and other investments.

This isn't a surefire way to making money in the market by any means, but it's a good place to start to figure out funds that are low-cost and decent for a beginning investor. There's an endless amount more on this you can learn. Start at places like the websites for CNNMoney (their Ultimate Guide to Retirement is helpful), Kiplinger.com, and Bankrate.

Help, I Don't Have an Employer-Offered Retirement Plan!

If your employer doesn't offer a retirement plan, or if you're self-employed, you will want to open your own retirement account. For many people, an IRA or a Roth IRA will be the right pick (see page 214 for explanations of these); but there are other options, too. My pick for where to do it: Vanguard. They have myriad low-cost investment options and if you have more than $50,000 to invest with them, you can use their financial adviser services.

An IRA is pretty simple to open: You can do it online or make a quick phone call to the company. Other options are Charles Schwab, T. Rowe Price, and Fidelity. Many of the same rules stated above apply to your IRA as to your 401(k). In 2017, the limit on what you can contribute to an IRA for people under fifty was $5,500 in a year; you can check IRS.gov for the latest figures. You'll then have to deposit money into your retirement account yourself each month. I recommend setting up regular automatic transfers into your IRA so you make sure you invest enough each year. You will typically have a ton of investment options, so if this feels overwhelming, remember that you can get a financial adviser to help make picks for you.

Here's an example of how you might figure out how much to set aside:

Goal

Contribute $5,500 to my Roth IRA.

When I Want to Achieve This Goal

1 year

How Much I Need to Save

$458 per month

My Plan to Save

- Have family dinner and a movie night at home instead of at the theater once a month. *Estimated savings: $147 ($46 for tickets, $25 for concessions, $76 for dinner).*
- Stop shopping at the mall for cute clothes, and just get what we really *need* at stores with better prices. *Estimated savings: $175 to $220.*
- Cancel gym membership (since we never actually go anyway!) and take a family walk instead: *Estimated savings: $100.*

Stop Letting Your Husband Make Your Retirement and Investing Decisions

As it turns out women tend to be better investors than men! One important study found that women's portfolios outperform men's by about one percentage point—which, depending on how much money they have invested, could amount to thousands of dollars! The reason, according to another study, is women tend to tinker with their investments less often than men.

Chapter 17

Managing All Your Money in Just 30 Minutes a Week

If your "clean" laundry drawer consists of multiple shirts with foodlike odors emanating from their crinkled fabric (at least you wiped the food chunks off with water, right?), the state of your living room is enough to make your partner consider signing you up for *Wife Swap*, and in an attempt to never have to do another dish again, you've convinced yourself that paper is the new ceramic, this chapter is for you! You're a mom who wants to get her finances under control, but just does not have the time to deal.

That's why my plan takes just thirty minutes to manage your money and move on. It probably takes you longer than that to clean the house, drive carpool, or do your grocery shopping. (Sorry, I can't help you there!) And you've already done a lot of the hard parts of managing your money: You now know what you owe each month in bills, debts, and insurance. And you know how much you need to save each month for emergencies and retirement. Now it's time to figure out how to pay and save for them—a must-do every month. And I'm going to make this as easy as possible! Managing your money shouldn't suck up more than about thirty minutes of your time each week. You'll be able to pay your bills, pay down debt, *and* save, plus ensure you've got your play money spending under control. Just follow the five simple steps in this chapter, and you're on your way to a secure financial future and having more fun with the money you do bring in.

Step 1: Get Two Free Checking Accounts

I know, you may think: I don't need two accounts, I'm on top of things! Just do it. I swear it makes this whole thing easier.

You probably already have one checking account, but get another. That's because, to streamline your financial life, I think it's best to have one account from which you pay for the five biggies we just covered: bills/essentials/basic living costs, debts, emergency, important savings, and insurance. The second account is for everything else. This system will keep things from getting messy. You won't spend bill money on extras you don't need, and it will be easier to keep track of your money when it isn't all lumped into one place. We moms just do not have time to clean up another mess!

Think this sounds weird? Think of it like this: People who run a small business keep their business and personal accounts separate. You can think of your two accounts the same way. One is for the "business" side of your life—the must-do stuff so you're on the right financial track. The second is for the "play" side of your life, those extras that make you happy like eating out with the family, or a mani-pedi.

We will talk about how much money goes in each account soon, but right now, just make sure you have two free checking accounts—and make sure they're free—so you can easily start implementing my plan. Then have the accounts linked, so you can transfer money between them as needed. (Just make sure that the banks allow you to transfer money between them for free, and remember that transfers can take a few days.)

Where to Find Free Checking Accounts

So your local bank doesn't have free checking—or it requires some insane minimum balance remain in your account to get free checking? Doesn't matter: There are now dozens of great online-only or primarily online banks that offer free checking with a lot more perks than your local bank. NerdWallet.com lists those with the best terms under its banking tab. I know you may be wondering: But what about ATM fees? The good news is, many have partnerships with local ATMs so you can get some withdrawals free, and some also offer ATM fee reimbursement. It is also worth checking your local credit union—these often have way better options than local banks—or joining one of the credit unions that lets nearly anyone join (Kiplinger has a good list of these).

Step 2: Set Up a Free Savings Account and an IRA (If Needed), If You Haven't Already

If you don't have high-interest debt, you're going to want to start saving. And you'll want a separate savings account to do that in.

For many people, retirement savings will be automatically deducted from your paycheck before you get that check, so you likely don't need a separate retirement account. If you do, open one such as an IRA. Everyone needs an emergency fund (aim for nine to twelve months or more of living expenses) and a free account to put that money in. See page 205 for details on what accounts make sense. You will automatically transfer your emergency and retirement savings (if applicable) from your bills and debts accounts (see Step 3 immediately below) into their respective savings/investment accounts each month. For those other goals we talk about in Chapter 19, you can transfer the savings into a separate savings account, or you can transfer it into your emergency savings account as long as you never spend your emergency savings on those other goals. Know that while it may seem like an emergency to escape to the Caribbean when it is twenty degrees out, I assure you, it is not!

Step 3: Set Up Your Bills and Debts Account

Choose one of your two free checking accounts to be your bills and debts account. This is where you're going to put all of your income for not just bills/essentials/basic living costs and debts, but also savings for emergencies and, if your employer doesn't deduct this right from your paycheck, for retirement. You'll also use this account for basic living costs (as discussed in Chapter 12) like groceries, essential clothing, gas, medicine, and school supplies; I recommend using the debit card linked to this account or cash from this account to pay for these items; or if you always pay in full, a rewards credit card that you use for your bills and debt payments. You will pay this credit card bill with the money from your bills and debts account.

If you get paid via direct deposit, you're going to split the direct deposit between the accounts, first putting what you need to pay your bills, debts, and life necessities in this account. The rest will go in your other "gravy" or "play money" checking account. If you don't have direct deposit, deposit the necessary money into your bills account, then deposit the amount you don't need for bills and debts into your play money account.

So how do you know how much you need to put into this account?

1. Use the charts you filled in on pages 176, 177, and 185 to complete the below chart. If you plan to or have made cuts to any of these expenses, use the new lower cost of that expense in this new chart. For the bills that are the same amount each month, this will be easy; simply put the amount owed each month. For

emergency savings, put the amount from your goals chart on page 205. If you save for retirement in the same way, the process will be the same. *Estimated time: 30 minutes.*

2. For things that vary, I'd recommend using the average you spent over the past twelve months last year and adding 10 to 15 percent to that monthly average for cushion. If you plan to or have made cuts to any of these expenses, use the new lower cost of that expense in this new chart. I also asked you to put the "highest" in that chart on page 176 just so you were aware that this bill could jump. (If one of the very high months is coming up really soon, be sure to account for that by putting in the money you need soon, since you may not have time this year to save up for it month by month.) *Estimated time: 30 minutes to 1 hour.*

3. You will also need to account for irregular bills in the coming year like taxes or insurance payments that are charged to you, say, yearly or twice yearly. Break down those bills into a cost per month. This way, you'll be putting a little each month into your "bills" account so that when the payment comes due, you have the money there. (If one of the irregular bills is coming up really soon, be sure to account for that by putting in the money you need soon, since you may not have time this year to save up for it month by month.) For things that are completely covered by your employer or deducted from your paycheck before tax (like life, health, disability insurance), just put zero. *Estimated time: 30 minutes.*

4. Not all items that are essential for your life are included in the following chart, but be sure to add in all your necessities. These might include essential car and home maintenance, HOA fees, work commuting costs, taxes you pay out of pocket, and alimony or child support.

5. For your debts, put the most you can pay on your highest interest debt in its box, then the minimum payment on all others in their respective boxes. *Estimated time: 30 minutes.*
6. Add these up, and you will see what your bills and debts cost you each month. That's how much money goes into your bills and debts checking account each month. *Estimated time: 30 minutes.*

What Your Bills and Debts Cost You Each Month

	What I'll Pay Each Month	Date Bill Is Due
Groceries		
Mortgage/rent		
Gas (home)		
Water		
Electricity		
Trash		
Phone		
Car payment		
Internet		
Homeowner's/ renter's insurance		
Car insurance		
Gas (car)		
Life insurance		

(Continued)

	What I'll Pay Each Month	Date Bill Is Due
Health insurance		
Regular medications and health care costs		
Essential clothing		
Disability insurance		
Student loan		
Credit card		
Childcare		
Essential toiletries		
Basic school supplies		
Emergency savings (will be transferred into savings account each month)		
Retirements savings (will be transferred into savings account each month)		
Taxes		
Other:		
TOTAL		

Step 4: Automate Payments

Now that you have this bills and debts account, you may want to make many of the payments for these bills and debts automatic so you can save yourself the hassle of writing checks or manually doing online payments. Automating the payments simply means setting up automatic payments from this bank account to the company you owe the money to. Your bank will usually require the payment details of the payee (name, zip code, address, account number, et cetera). You can also do this the reverse way (as long as the company you are working with is reputable like a big-name mortgage or utility company) whereby you give the company your banking information and the company deducts the money from your account each month. Beware, of course, of giving banking information to anyone other than major lenders or utility companies. And know that there is a risk in automating payments (as there is a risk of doing any shopping online) but to me, the convenience outweighs the low risk of fraud.

1. Set up automatic electronic payments from your bills and debts checking account on a set date to each company, or you can do it the reverse way as discussed above. Do this for the bills and debts that are the same amount each month. If you have, say, credit card debt on multiple cards, it's smart to have all of them set to autopay at least the minimum (and more on that super high interest one). *Estimated time: 30 minutes.*

2. For bills that are in irregular amounts, you risk overdraft if you autopay, so I recommend you do electronic payments to those companies by entering those payments each month by hand in the specified amount. I prefer electronic payments to mailing a check just because, well you know, the U.S. Postal Service. *Estimated time: 15 minutes a week.*

3. Set up a monthly automatic electronic transfer for the emergency and retirement savings from your bills and debts account to their proper savings and retirement accounts each month. If you're also saving for something special—like a career shift to part-time work or a lower-paying but lovable career, an epic family vacation, or your dream home, you might want to set up a similar transfer from your gravy money account to a special savings account for that goal. *Estimated time: 15 minutes.*

4. Link your gravy money account and this bills and debts accounts in case of emergency. There may be times when a bill is sky high for whatever reason and you will need to move money from your gravy account to this account to cover it. *Estimated time: 15 to 30 minutes.*

Step 5: Do Thirty-Minute Weekly Check-ins

Every week, you need to check in on your financial situation for about half an hour. It may take you longer when you first start doing it, but you will get the hang of this and it will start taking less and less time. You can do it whenever—as long as you set the time on your calendar and stick to it no matter what. I recommend setting aside this time on a Google Calendar and have it automatically remind you with an email and a pop-up notification that this is going to happen on X night at X time so you can't forget.

These weekly check-ins are designed to a) ensure all your bills and debts are paid in a timely manner (and that all automatic payments went through), and b) give you a status update on where you stand with your "play" money. And there are only three things you need to do:

1. Deal with bills and debt payments

I recommend paying bills every other week, if possible. The twice monthly bill paying sessions are better than paying bills whenever they come in because 1) you're not likely to forget to pay bills, and 2) it takes less time to handle them in a group than one at a time. Rather than find a bill, get your checkbook or log in to your account, and avoid the distractions of all the other things you notice you need to do in the process, you just do it twice a month. It doesn't seem like much, but over time, all that scrambling to pay as bills come in adds up to hours of time that you've simply wasted. No thanks!

Do your thirty-minute money check-ins at the same day and time each week, if possible. On the sessions that fall on the middle of the month and at the end of the month, pay bills and check to make sure your automatically set bills (including savings) were sent and paid. Plus, at these sessions, you should check in on your spending from your bills and debts account. At this point, you should have this kind of spending well under control so it should be a very short check-in; remember that in most months there will be money left in this account. It will stay there from month to month to account for months when a bill might be higher (like in winter or summer for utilities) or when an irregular bill (like insurance) might hit.

To make sure you don't miss any bills, all you need is a handy checklist.

1. Using a sheet of paper or a Google Doc, make a list of all of your bills and debts.
2. Divide the list into two smaller lists: one for payments due by the middle of the month and one for payments due by the end of the month (or the first of the next month). If there are debts that don't fit into the timing of this, make a note of those, too.

3.   Note on your list which you've set up as automatic payment and which you have to pay yourself.

By using this list, the entire bill paying and account check-in process, once you get the hang of it, should take a max of twenty minutes—mostly because you've automated so much of it! Just log in to your bank account, make sure those bills are paid, pay those that aren't automated, do a quick glace to make sure you haven't overspent on something like groceries or that a bill wasn't super high for an unknown reason, and done!

Sometimes, you'll have a big imbalance when bills need to be paid (like way more at the end of the month than the middle of the month). In that case, it may make sense to pay some of them a bit earlier, if you can, so you don't have too many to deal with at any given time. So, if you know a bill is a set amount each month pay it earlier so that is one thing off your checklist. Also, make sure to note on your calendar which of your weekly money sessions are for bills; this way you'll never forget to pay them again!

The only thing that might, at first, seem strange to you is that you also pay for groceries (but not eating out), essential clothing, basic school supplies, and things like medicines from this account. (If something happens, like an essential medication is needed that is crazy expensive, it's important to remember that you may have to do something like put it on your credit card and them immediately transfer money from your emergency savings account to your bills and debts account to cover this credit card bill before its due.) This is the only "bill" that you won't deal with in these sessions; you'll just pay for these with your debit card or a certain amount of cash or in some cases (like if you always pay your bill on time and in full) with a rewards credit card. Any extras—dinners out, snacks on the go, a beautiful new scarf—are paid for out of your gravy money account.

2. Check In on Your "Gravy" Money

Every week at your weekly check-in, you need to see where you stand with your "play" or "gravy" money. This is the number one way to prevent yourself from going into debt (or more debt). (We will talk about how much money to put into this account in Chapter 18, but for now just know that checking in on this account is part of your weekly check-in.) Remain aware of your weekly play money-spending goal throughout the week, but you don't need to keep a running tally of every dollar you spend. You also don't have to go in and check that account unless you really feel the urge or think your spending is creeping up on you; though you may want to do a midweek glance if you feel you've lost track. If you know you made a splurge on say a dinner out, scrimp for a few days following. It's not always perfect, but it works well enough to keep your spending way more under control than it is now! You can use Mint (or another app) to help you even more with this—they have a feature that will email you with your weekly spending broken out by category; link your gravy money account to Mint and your check-in will be a cinch. In these sessions, you also want to make sure that any automatic savings to your fun goals went through.

At the end of the week during your weekly meeting, check your bank account and see how much over or under your target you are. If you use credit cards, you will also have to look at your credit card statement and see what you spent there and pay that bill from your bank account. You should also know that it is fine to have NO credit cards. Yes, there are perks to having them (particularly if you pay them off in full each month and can earn cash rewards for using them), but if they lead you into debt, just say NO. There is no reason to hold a slice of temptation in your wallet if you don't think you can handle it. This whole check-in should take twenty minutes or less.

If you spent too much this week, make a concrete plan to cut back next week. This shouldn't take you long. Unless you went way overboard, you can usually pick one thing to cut back on and that will do the trick. In addition to the savings tips throughout this book, a Google search on how to save money will yield you hundreds of ideas, but really the rule is easy—before you pull out your wallet for anything in that budget week, pause for ten seconds and ask yourself, *Do I really need this?* You will be surprised how often the answer is no. Put the item down and move on.

3. Find Ways to Boost Debt Payments or Savings

As noted earlier, two weeks a month you will spend part of your thirty-minute session paying bills. In the two weeks when you're not paying bills, you will spend part of the session looking for ways to pay down your debt faster or increase your savings. When you scan through your "play money" spending, what do you see that you keep doing that is frivolous? Let's say you go out to dinner four times per month—would you really miss it if you cut that down to three? Then you can add an additional $50 to the money you send your credit card company each month. Do you go to a certain store a lot and overspend there? Try making a list of what you need before you go, and sticking to those items only. If you (or your kids!) didn't need it before you saw it, you probably don't need it. It's all about looking at your spending patterns and identifying the things you spend money on that a) you might be able to spend less on or to spend less often on, or b) the things you buy that aren't needed or aren't really making you happier.

Rules to Keep You on Track

The plan is pretty straightforward, right? But since life has a tendency to get in the way of our best intentions, here are a few tips that will help you stick with it.

* **Pick a specific time once a week to do your budget check-in.**

It should be the same time every week, when the kids are away or asleep and you have no distractions. Have your partner join you if you have one. I suggest you set aside one hour at first. Once you get used to it, these sessions will likely only take thirty minutes, sometimes you may need a little more time, sometimes a little less.

* **Put this time on your calendar and send a reminder to yourself.**

Don't start avoiding these weekly check-ins or you can and will go back to your previous willy-nilly spending. I not only have the time blocked out in my Google calendar, but I send myself a reminder to attend my own meeting—just in case things get crazy around my house.

Why This Approach Works

Budgets that are too strict—where you have to keep track of everything you spend daily—simply don't work for most people. It's just too hard to fit that into your daily life. My approach is more like a reasonable weight-loss plan—it's okay to splurge sometimes, as long as you then make other cutbacks accordingly. I also think it's essential that once a week, you really go through your spending for that week to make sure you're within your weekly threshold. Many other budgets have you do it monthly, but that is too seldom. I don't think most people can stay on track with their budgets if they're only really checking in once a month.

Sample Schedule for Weekly Money Check-ins

Week 1	Weekly play money spending check-in/tweak next week's spending accordingly if needed.	Find a way to pay down debt faster/boost savings, and briefly check in on bills/debts account spending.
Week 2	Weekly play money spending check-in/tweak next week's spending accordingly if needed.	Deal with bills/debts payments, and briefly check in on bills/debts account spending.
Week 3	Weekly play money spending check-in/tweak next week's spending accordingly if needed.	Find a way to pay down debt faster/boost savings, and briefly check in on bills/debts account spending.
Week 4	Weekly play money spending check-in/tweak next week's spending accordingly if needed.	Deal with bills/debts payments, and briefly check in on bills/debts account spending.

You'll want to revisit this plan as your financials change—say you pay off a big debt and now have more to save, or you get hit with a huge car repair and have to dip into your emergency savings. That may take a few hours when that happens. But for now, I'm not going to dwell on those things. All I'm going to say is major congrats! This is a huge step forward in your financial life—and one that will positively impact your whole family for years to come.

Chapter 18

When Mama Gets Hers

Maximizing Your "Gravy" Money

Now that we've dealt with saving for emergencies and retirement, paying down debt, and paying bills and you've got your money under control, let's get to the best part: spending your "gravy" or play money! This is the money that will allow you to whisk the family off to Key West, sign up for a series of yoga classes or a deep tissue massage or two, or hire a cleaning lady every couple weeks so you can get a break. It's your reward for doing the hard part. I wish I could just say, "Spend it however you like!" But I wouldn't be doing you any favors if I didn't point out that there are a few catches.

First, sometimes you'll need to spend your gravy money on things that aren't exactly as fun as a Key West vacation or a dinner out with the family. For example, new sports equipment for the kids' extracurriculars, or clothes you didn't exactly budget for in your "bills and debts" accounts. Your kids have a way of losing a tennis shoe or breaking a racket just when you were hoping to finally put away an extra $200 into savings, don't they? Most of these things don't qualify for the emergency fund, but your kids may not agree with that. So you'll want to put them first when you're thinking about spending that gravy money because they're obviously good for your family. It's a good idea to have a debit card linked to your gravy money checking account. Though if you always pay your credit card on time in full, it may make sense to have a rewards credit card, and pay the bill from your gravy money account.

The rest of the money is for you and the fam to enjoy. But in this, too, I have an opinion—don't I always!—and it's that you should probably spend the money in a way that will make you and your family happy. I know as well as anyone that it may seem like buying your daughter that adorable dress at Nordstrom will make you (and her) happy, but that's probably not true. So, in the next section, I'm going to talk about how to spend to boost your and your family's happiness. Of course, you don't have to listen to me: This is YOUR gravy money, and you can spend it how you wish. Once you've paid for all the stuff you need to from the Quick Guide the rest is all yours!

Know How Much You'll Have in Your Gravy Money Account Each Month

Before we talk about how to spend to boost your happiness, you first need to know how much money you'll be putting into this gravy money account each month. The calculation to figure out what goes into your gravy account is pretty simple: It's the leftover money that isn't going into the bills and debts account. For example, if you have $1,200 left after paying all your bills and setting aside your savings, that's about $300 a week. You can do (pretty much) whatever the heck you want with that $300. I adore taking the family out to dinner, but that's just me!

The Happiness Project: A Spending Philosophy

Your day-to-day spending philosophy should be simple: It's love, not material things, that matter most—and as J.Lo says "love don't cost a thing!" But what you do buy can impact your happiness, and there's plenty of research about what kinds of purchases make people happy, so I'm going to break them down here. But first, I have to say this: Do not—I repeat DO NOT—go into debt to buy any of these things. Having credit card debt, research shows, makes us stressed and unhappy, while working toward financial security provides contentment. So, here's how to spend your gravy money for maximum happiness.

1. **Spend on experiences, not things.** Research shows that spending on experiences—a vacation with the family, a concert with the kids—makes you a lot happier than spending it on material things like an iPad, clothes, or a TV. But people often rationalize that material things last longer so they must give us more happiness; that's simply not true. The memories from an experience give us happiness long after that experience is complete. And you can have plenty of experiences without spending a dime: a dance party or camping in your yard with the kids, for example, and you don't need to spend thousands to have a great vacation or other experience.

2. **Spend on more little things rather than one big thing.** You'll get more happiness by buying more little things frequently—hello morning Starbucks!—than you will from one larger purchase like a big-screen TV or a fancy car. Of course, you can't go crazy buying little things all the time (a daily morning coffee from the store, for example, will cost you about $675 a year) but it's safe to say that buying yourself

a small treat each week or a couple times a week is going to give you more happiness than buying one big thing for yourself every few months. These are just tiny little bursts of joy that brighten each day.

3. **Spend on others instead of yourself.** Okay, I'm not saying you need to be a saint (I'm not one myself! Hello twice a year spa visits to decompress!) but in general, spending on others has been proven to make you happier than spending on yourself. That can mean giving money to causes you care about, or simply spending on dear friends or family. I try to do a little of both: Give what I can to the charities I care about (I can't resist a good animal rescue cause!) and also to my family. I have automated my daughter's college savings and I look at her 529 account regularly and imagine her in a cap and gown when I do it. Few things make me feel happier in life than that little moment each month, knowing that I am changing her life by being able to pay for a lot of her college costs.

4. **Spend on things that give you more time with your friends and family or to do things you enjoy.** We get a bigger emotional benefit from spending time with friends and family or doing things that we love than doing something like, say, housework. So if you're in a toss-up situation between buying the family a new big-screen TV or hiring a cleaning service twice a month, hire the cleaning service, and then make sure to spend the time you would have spent cleaning with your friends or family or doing a hobby or activity you love.

5. **Take your time before making big purchases.** If you are going to buy something big, even if it's a material thing, know that you derive a lot of pleasure from the anticipation of the event, so wait to buy that item for weeks or months if you can. Imagine how much you'll all enjoy that vacation

as you're planning it! Not only is this what a smart shopper does anyway, it's a sneaky way to boost your happiness because you get more time to look forward to the event or purchase.

No matter what you own, it's important to take a few minutes at least once a week to think about how grateful you are for what you have. We very quickly adapt to purchases like a new home or car and start wanting more, which creates unhappiness. Resist this urge with weekly "gratitude meditations." I know, it sounds hokey, but it's really important for our happiness—and to keep our spending down—that we appreciate what we have so we don't suddenly start coveting more. Put time on your calendar for this. Sit in a quiet room and simply write down all the things—be they family or your wonderful home—that you are grateful for. Keep a notebook of these things and refer to it when you start down the whole "I need to keep up with the Joneses" routine.

And here's another secret I love: Many of the things that make us happiest are free or cost very little. Researchers at Princeton do a huge survey of thousands of people called the Princeton Affect and Time Survey and found that the following activities make us happiest in life—with playing with our kids coming in at number one.

15 Activities That Make Us Happiest

1. Playing with kids
2. Listening to music
3. Hunting, fishing, boating, and/or hiking
4. Attending a sporting event
5. Going to a party or reception
6. Doing sports or exercising

7. Purchasing personal services
8. Travel
9. Going to a café or bar
10. Participating in religious activities/worship
11. Walking
12. Talking to others or having a phone or text chat
13. Caring for older kids
14. Eating meals and snacks
15. Relaxing, thinking, doing nothing

What makes us least happy? Some of the items at the bottom of the list are going to the doctor or getting medical care, setting the table/washing dishes, and doing laundry and ironing. I know, I know—some of those things are inevitable in life, but the lesson here is that if you can find ways to do these things more efficiently, do it!

4 Simple Productivity Hacks for Work and Home That Will Give You More Time with the Kids

The number one thing that makes us happy is playing with the kids. So here's how to find more time to do that!

1. Make it about helping them.

   Research shows that when you do a favor for someone, they are far more likely to happily, and willingly do one for you. That's why you get so many of those return address labels in the mail—the company knows that giving you that gift makes you more likely to donate to their cause. The same principle works for your boss. If you know you're going to need time off, a week or so before you ask, make sure you do them a favor—take a project off their hands, for example, or be the one to arrange a couple of meetings. This way, a request to leave early for your kid's play or soccer game is likely to be met with a non-begrudging yes. It sounds simple, but the psychological pull of needing to return favors is so strong that this is one of the most effective strategies out there for moms.

2. Stop wasting so much time on email.

    First, you must avoid "the skim and skip." Most of us skim a bunch of emails and then mark them as "unread" or "to be dealt with later" nearly every day of our working lives. But this can double the amount of time it takes you to deal with each one because you're reading each twice—once initially and another time when you answer the email—*and* thinking about what to do about them twice. Instead, it's better to set aside specific times of day for dealing with every email you need to right then (even if this means 10 minutes each hour, if you have one of those jobs where people want answers quickly), and then moving on to whatever else you need to do and taking a break from email entirely. Furthermore, this helps boost productivity in another way: By preventing you from constantly looking at your email and thus interrupting your flow on other projects (which research shows make them take longer).

    It's also not a bad idea to strategically schedule emails. All right, this will raise some eyebrows, but it works. Honestly, I do it because our on-24/7 work culture is insane to me! About once a week, before you leave the office, schedule an email or two to go out later in the evening or super early in the morning, which creates the appearance of a works-around-the-clock employee. I schedule emails for around 9 p.m., and then check my email on my phone in bed at 9:30 before I go to sleep (yes, 9:30 is about as late as I can stay awake these days!) to see if there's a response. If there is, I write back something like: "I'll come find you in the morning to discuss," effectively ending the back and forth. I sometimes do the same thing for 6:30 a.m. emails, check for a response at 7, and then write the same response.

3. Follow the "rule of 6" for your daily to-do list.

Most to-do lists have twenty-plus items on them, but research shows people are more likely to get things done when presented with six choices max rather than a laundry list of twenty-four or thirty choices. So, mom's daily "to-do" lists should have a maximum of six total items on them. You can have a longer list for long-term goals, but each day, your list should be six or fewer items. Add each item on your list to an online/ smartphone calendar with a time period blocked out for each item. Factor in the fact that you will have interruptions from the kids and others when blocking out that time, and set automatic reminders for when you need to switch gears. Google's online calendar is free and makes it easy to set multiple reminders.

Block out certain times of day for "administrative" tasks like checking email or answering calls, changing the laundry, or making a quick dinner for the kids. And don't fall into the Martha Stewart trap of feeling the need to make the "perfect" dinner, make up everyone's bed with hospital corners, or dust more than once a week. Seriously, Martha has so much more help than you! Plus your kids would rather have chicken fingers for dinner and no one's eating off the freaking fan blades so let 'em be.

Schedule the hardest task first thing in the morning. Each day, reward yourself for completing your mini to-do list with something small like letting yourself watch your favorite show after the kids go to bed. This gives you a treat to look forward to—and motivation for getting all that stuff done!

4. Prep a list of ready-made "no" excuses.

You've no doubt heard this before, but because of how important it is to managing your time better, I'm going to repeat it: Just say no. Say no to everything from making homemade cookies for the bake sale to having a two-hour lunch with that alpha mom you don't totally love.

To do this, first make a list of the priority people in your life, and put your family (including yourself!) at the top. Then rank the people in your life according to importance to you—and don't forget to put yourself high up on that list!

After that, think back to the past week and what you were doing each hour of the day—be it laundry, dishes, carpool, or coffee with friends—and whom you're doing the task "for" (i.e., does it benefit you, your family, a friend?). At the end of the week, review this log. What you find may shock you. How many of those things were things that didn't need to be done, things you should have said no to but instead said yes to? How many of those things took far longer than they should have? How often were people of lower priority monopolizing your time?

You can then pick at least one thing to stop doing entirely. Look to cut items that a) aren't focused on your priority people (seriously, your child doesn't need you to head the PTA to feel loved); and b) can easily be outsourced. Your husband may not do the dishes as well as you do, but that's totally fine! And if you can afford to hire a pro, do it. Look at inexpensive services like TaskRabbit.com to outsource things like dry cleaning and other errands. In two months, pick another thing to stop doing entirely—and on and on until your list is pared down enough to give you me time.

If you still struggle to say no, make a mental list of ready-made excuses. When put on the spot, many of us default to yes. So have a no excuse handy that you've practiced and memorized. It can be anything from "I wish I could, but my house is a disaster so today isn't great" to "It's my busy season at work so I barely have any free time, these days, ugh!"

What's more, for the things you do say yes to, make strict time limits. Let friends know that while you value their friendship, you can't spend two hours over coffee every single day. It's totally not personal, you're just on a quest to finally tackle your never-ending to-do list. If that seems really uncomfortable (and it can be) make up an excuse for somewhere else you have to be, even set an alarm on your phone in advance, and get going!

5 Ways to Enrich Your Children's Lives Without Spending a Dime

Obviously, you love your kids to pieces—that's the number one, two, and three ways to enrich their lives. But I know you're doing that already! So here are five ways (proven with research!) that parents can enrich their children's lives.

1. **Volunteer often as a family.** Make helping others a regular part of your family's schedule, be it once a week or once a month, whatever you can fit in. Use VolunteerMatch.org to find opportunities in your area.
2. **Ask the kids to perform regular random acts of kindness.** Weekly, ask your kids to perform a "random act of kindness."

It can be anything from making a surprise visit to Grandma to texting something nice to a friend. Anything that will make another person feel good. Doing this, research shows, also has the benefit of making your kids feel good themselves.

3. **Give your kids plenty of unstructured playtime.** Many kids today have so many activities that they barely get any time to play as they want to. One study found that kids today have eight fewer hours a week of unstructured playtime than we did as kids. But research shows unstructured playtime boosts creativity and can improve emotional intelligence and social skills. (Plus, it gives mama some free time to herself!)

4. **Get out in nature more often.** Take a family hike, go on a camping trip—whatever you do, research shows that getting out in nature reduces anxiety and stress. And with all the homework and activities kids have today, it's more important than ever that you make sure your kids have enough trees in their lives.

5. **Encourage and support friendships.** Fact: Kids with good friends are happier. As a parent, it's essential you support their friendships by asking about their friends' lives, encouraging them to have friends over, doing activities with friends, and doing kind things for their friends. Don't push too hard but let it be known that friendships are important and something your child should cultivate and cherish.

Chapter 19

Saving for the Fun Stuff (and Getting a Raise While You're at It!)

Some of the things that make us happiest—like taking a vacation with friends or family, for example—require a little saving before we can afford to buy them. And that's what this chapter is all about: how to save for your goals beyond emergencies and retirement. You might be saving for a down payment on a dream home. Hello, finally getting your white-picket fence! Maybe you want to send your kid to an awesome summer camp. Or perhaps your daydream of finally getting to take a solo yoga retreat—no phones, no kids, nothing but pure silence and Zen! I'm currently dreaming of this one myself… This chapter will walk you through how to create a list of goals, figure out their cost, and start saving for them.

Step 1: Start Dreaming and Turn Those Dreams into a Goals List

I want you to think about what kinds of things you want to achieve both for your family and yourself that will make you happier. But I have one rule: As you make this list, remember that it's not enough to just make goals for your family's happiness, you MUST make at least one for yourself. I'd recommend something you think will make you a happier person. A number of studies show that moms who are unhappy—even though they don't mean to—tend to have a negative impact on their children. Remember, what you do to make yourself happy doesn't have to cost much. If you're stuck on how to get happy, look at the list in the last chapter for inspiration. A simple way may be spending time with your kids, getting outside and boating or hiking, going to a sporting event, or listening to music.

Come up with a list of three to five goals for you and your family, and once you've made your list, note which will cost money. *Estimated time: 1 hour.*

Step 2: Prioritize Your Goals

Put your goals in order of the one you most want to achieve and then on down. Now that you have an idea of how much you have in your "gravy" money fund, you will likely have an idea of how much you can reasonably put into savings each week. Most likely, you won't be able to save for all of your goals at once. If that's the case, prioritize the one or two that are most important to you. If you can save for all of these at once, good for you! *Estimated time: 30 minutes.*

Step 3: Price Out Your Goals

Once you know which of your goals you need to save for, you'll have to price them out. For example, for something like a trip to Hawaii, you're going to need to know the cost of flights, hotels, meals, transportation around the island, tours, and spending money to put a total price on your trip. Doing this will likely take about an hour per goal, sometimes less if it's a simple goal, sometimes more if it's something like a big vacation. But block one hour a day to find out the cost of each of your goals. *Estimated time: 1 hour per goal.*

Step 4: Figure Out How Much to Save Each Week to Make It Happen

Think about when you want to achieve this goal and then do the math on how much you will need to save to make that happen. Let's say your Hawaii vacation comes to $5,000 and you want to book this trip a year from now. You will need to save an extra $417 each month (the total cost of the trip divided by twelve) to have enough to pay for the trip in twelve months. Sites like Bankrate.com and Mint.com have calculators that can help. Revise accordingly—like if you realize you can never save that much every week, extend the timeline of your goal and redo the math. You might also want to look at ways to make the goal less expensive. Perhaps a different time of year has better rates or lower airfares, for example. *Estimated time: 15 to 30 minutes per goal.*

Step 5: Make a Plan for How to Save That Money Each Week

Brainstorm ideas of how you can set extra money aside. You can use your weekly check-ins on your gravy money to continue working on this. You can also flip back to page 203, where we tackle emergency savings, for some suggestions on how to save each week. For even more ideas, there are tons of great resources online; a simple "easy ways to save money" Google search will yield plenty of results. *Estimated time: 1 to 2 hours per goal.*

	Total cost of this goal	When you can achieve this goal	How much you need to save each week to achieve goal	Plan to save that much each week
Goal 1:				
Goal 2:				
Goal 3:				
Goal 4:				
Goal 5:				
Goal 6:				

Sample Goals Chart

6 Psychological Tricks to Help You Spend Less—So You Can Save More!

1. Train Your Brain

We often overspend because of emotions—we've had a rough day and feel we deserve to treat ourselves, we're too tired to deal with cooking, et cetera. You wake up in the morning certain that you'll be a spending angel, but by the end of the day, you're swiping your card to fix those feelings. To stop this pattern, you need to insert a step in between the *This day is horrible. I'm tired. [Insert spending trigger here]* and *So I'm buying this right now*. Imagine a very specific savings goal as this middle step. Training your brain to think about that long-term savings goal—something you really want, like a trip to Europe or horseback riding lessons for your daughter—will help you curb the short-term spending.

2. Put Your Specific Money Goals in Writing—and Carry Them with You Everywhere You Go

Budgets often fail because we lose sight of what's important. Carry a list of your money goals—like paying for college or getting to go to London with your hubs—in your wallet, right beside that credit card. Frankly, it's a helpful (though an admittedly none-too-subtle) reminder to ask yourself *Do I really need that?* before you make an impulse purchase. Psychologists say the more specific you make these goals, the more effective they will be—so add in a timeline in which you want to make it happen, and any other details you think will help you remember that those savings or that trip are far more important than that muffin and coffee.

Living on Less Gives You More—More for Your Family, More for Yourself

You spend less now, you can afford to send the kids to summer camp or to college. You spend less now, you pay down your debts more quickly and can live a more full life—filled with less stress and anxiety. It's about spending less in the moment, so that your life is better down the road. That's a trade-off I know you are willing to make! Write your version of this down and carry it with you everywhere. I guarantee you that cute handbag at Marshall's is nothing compared to a future happy family and self!

---

3. Get Social Support

We often bust our budget in social situations—a nice dinner out with the moms, for example. That's why, when I'm trying to save big, I remind my friends that I'm cutting back this month to try to save for something. Say it ahead of time, before you even go out (we don't want any awkward bill talk at the table!) and your budget can help shape the plans to something cheaper or free. One study found that people who kept their New Year's resolutions—including money-related ones—did three things: They wrote down their goals, they wrote out a specific plan for making them happen (e.g., I will save $100 a week by doing X, Y, and Z each week), and they had a friend hold them accountable. Each week, they checked in with the friend and told them about their progress. Indeed, 76 percent of people who did all three of these things had either achieved or were on track to achieve their goals, versus less than half who just thought about their goals.

4. Put in the Time If You Want to Turn Frugality into a Habit

The old rule that it takes twenty-one days to make something a habit simply isn't true; it seems to have come from a book from the 1960s and new research shows that that "rule" isn't legit. The study, published in 2009 in the *European Journal of Social Psychology*, revealed that it takes people sixty-six days, on average, of doing something each day before it becomes a habit.

5. Allow the Occasional Splurge

Frankly, this is the only way most people will ever stick to a budget. If you've kept to your spending goals all week, allow yourself to get a mani-pedi or a dinner out. Plan this splurge (I love to do it on the weekend as a treat) and use it to reward yourself. Remembering all week that if you meet your spending goals you will get this treat will help you keep with your spending plan. And getting the reward will make it feel like a budget isn't totally depriving you.

6. Abandon Black-and-White Thinking

We've all done it—been super diligent about spending less, gotten fed up, and then blown our budget. Some of us then think: *Well I screwed it all up so what's the point in even trying anymore.* In psychology, that's called "black-and-white thinking" and it's a death trap for your financial goals. To combat it, stop focusing so much on the thing you bought that blew your budget and instead focus on all the ways that you spent and saved responsibly that week. There are almost always way more of those moments than big splurges.

A Simple Way to Stay Motivated to Keep Saving: Chart Your Progress

This tip is from my amazing editor Christina, who's pretty fabulous at saving money herself. She makes a little chart using Excel in regular increments, say $100, all leading up toward her goal of say $1,000. She posts it right by her desk. Every time she transfers $100 to savings, she colors in a $100 box on the chart with highlighter so she can actually see her progress and stay motivated. "It also helps to battle online spending sprees, when you see that chart in your peripheral vision," she jokes.

Making Saving a Family Affair

Saving money shouldn't just fall on mom and dad—it's also a good opportunity to teach the kids about money and have them chip in.

One easy way is to create a big family goal that everyone is excited about, say a trip to the beach. When the kids ask if they can have something at the store, remind them that you're saving for this awesome trip and that giving up this small treat now means they get to go on that vacation, which is way more exciting anyway. This is a simple lesson in delaying gratification. If they're a bit older, you can also have them save for a fun event—say a trip to an amusement park—that will happen on that vacation. Have them save a percentage of their allowance each week (see page 263 for general advice about allowances) to put toward admission and souvenirs.

So You Want to Quit Your Job or Go Part-Time for a Few Years...

For many moms, saving for the fun stuff means getting to spend way more time having fun with the kids—aka getting to quit their jobs or go part-time! But can you afford to do that? Of course, there's the basic math—how able the family is to live without your income each month, which is relatively straightforward. Look at what giving up your income would mean for your family's ability to pay bills and debts and still save. But, there are a few other things you need to think about before you make the decision to say sayonara to work.

For Florida mom Amanda Base, a marketing coordinator, the birth of her second child presented a big dilemma for her and her husband. The cost of childcare became "as much as a mortgage payment...more than I paid for college tuition" and would mean that much of her salary was eaten up by those costs, she explains. She asked herself: "Do I work to break even on costs and further my career, and increase my earning potential? Or do I leave the workforce and risk my career taking a hit?" Ultimately, the couple decided that Amanda would go to work so she could continue building up her earnings and career. Has it been easy? No—and she says some days she feels like she isn't doing either work or family that well—but ultimately, she says that for her, it's worth it because she didn't want to "be entry-level again in my forties." "It's hard and I have to get creative to make it work," she says. "But it's right for us."

Whether to work or stay at home is a personal decision, unique to each couple or parent, and working or not working is right for some and not others. I know tons of stay-at-home moms that wouldn't trade that job for anything! But it is important to know financially what quitting your job—even for just a few years—will really mean. And it's not just a salary hit.

When you quit your job, your finances—and future finances—take a triple hit. 1) You don't get your salary for the years you are out of the workforce; 2) Even when you return, your salary is likely to never go as high as those who'd never quit; 3) You likely aren't contributing to Social Security or your 401(k) and getting the benefits of matching and compounding. Consider the example of a woman who starts working at twenty-two, and at twenty-six (when she's making $50,000 a year) decides to leave the workforce for three years to raise her child. That three-year career pause would cost her $506,000, according to data from the nonpartisan policy institute Center for American Progress (CAP). Why is it $500,000 and not $150,000? The $150,000 is just her lost wages over those three years. But she also gives up lost retirement and Social Security contributions ($158,000 over the life of her career, assuming she retires at sixty-six) and lost future wage growth ($198,000).

Want to know how much it would cost you, personally, to take a few years off work? The Center for American Progress has an incredible calculator that will do just that for you: Visit interactives .americanprogress.org/childcarecosts (or just google: "Center for American Progress lifetime child care calculator").

Bottom line: You have to think about more than your salary when you think about taking a career pause. But that doesn't mean you shouldn't do it. For many of us, getting to spend 24/7 with our babies, even if it's just for a few years, is far more important than money. You might have to work many years longer than you'd planned to be able to retire, but that may certainly be a trade that you're willing to take.

The "Mommy Penalty" (and How to Combat It by Getting a Fat Raise)

The really frustrating thing is that even if you DO stay in the workforce, you'll likely be penalized just for being a mom. Yes, it's absolutely unfair, but it's true. Moms get paid less than women who aren't moms, even when you consider experience and other factors. While dads get a boost when they have children, one study showed women take a 7 percent per child hit by becoming a mom. Other studies show a roughly 5 percent penalty. Either way, over a lifetime, that's tens of thousands of dollars in lost earnings.

The best thing you can do to combat this is to ask for the raises you deserve. If you've been at the job for a year or more without a raise—or have recently taken on more responsibilities—you should consider asking for a raise. Typically raises are given about once a year, often in conjunction with an annual review. Here are some tips on how best to ask for a raise:

* **Come armed with info on how awesome you are.** Make a list of all the things that you do on the job, your biggest successes. Bring a portfolio of your best work and be specific, and if you can somehow quantify these, even better (like saying you "increased revenue by X percent by doing X").

It's important to practice how you will talk about each item beforehand so you don't stumble or seem insecure about how great you are.

* **Know how much to ask for.** This is one of the hardest things to know. Start on sites like Glassdoor.com and PayScale .com to see if you're getting paid what others in your field do, though these sites are sometimes too general. It's often better, if you know people, to talk to others in the industry about what jobs in your city and industry pay. You may even want to go on a few interviews, even if you aren't 100 percent sure you want a new job, as that can a) provide you an idea of what other companies pay, and b) could yield an offer that you could take to your boss to beat. This may take five or so hours of your time, but could yield you thousands of dollars extra in salary a year—totally worth it! Another thing you can do is scour job postings for jobs like yours; though they don't always include salary, some do (or at least a salary range). Combining these methods will likely yield you at least a rough idea of what you should be paid. The other thing to note is what a "typical" raise looks like. If you're asking for a raise along with a promotion, that's typically accompanied by a 10 to 20 percent uptick in salary. If you're just asking for raise but without a different job, 1 to 5 percent is typical. Ask for a little more than you think you'll get.

* **Frame the number in the right way.** Research shows that if you give a range with the low number as your actual target raise and the high number as something even better, you're more likely to get what you want. So let's say you want to make $55,000. You might say you were thinking of a salary of between $55,000 to $60,000.

* **Make an early morning appointment with the boss—and avoid Mondays and Fridays.** Several studies show that

mornings are the best time to ask for a raise, for a few reasons, one being that people tend to be more moral in the morning. Plus, at most jobs, the stress builds throughout the day as responsibilities pile up. It's also a good idea to avoid asking for a raise on a Monday (because, frankly, Mondays are when people are at their grumpiest) or a Friday, when the boss just wants to get out the door.

* **Negotiation is about more than just money.** Of course, the money is nice, but maybe your company just isn't in a position to give it. So think about what else they could give you to get you to a place you want to be: a day or two where you work from home, more vacation days, different or flexible hours, a performance bonus, extra pay for taking on additional tasks. Rank these priorities before you go in for a salary negotiation; if you hear a final no on the raise, these might be worth bringing up.

* **Don't let a no scare you off.** If you get rejected, ask for the opportunity to revisit the raise in the future. Ask for a list of things you can do in the coming year to have more of a chance of getting a raise.

Giving Kids the Money Lessons They Need for the Future

Giving your kids money when they ask—no strings attached—isn't a great idea for your budget, or for them learning to manage money. In fact, one of the best ways to protect your kids from debt and other financial mishaps later in life—which frankly you could be cleaning up well into your sixties and seventies—is to teach them about money now, by doing things like giving them an allowance. I know, talking about money isn't comfortable for a lot of people, but the first thing to understand is that money is an uncomfortable topic for most people, so you're not alone. I always think of it like this: I'm doing my daughter a favor—a big one!—by teaching her about money, including where it comes from and how to save it. I know this from personal experience: Frankly, I wish my parents had taught me about the topic! I might have avoided a pile of credit card debt in my twenties—when I barely understood the concept of compound interest—had they done that. I vaguely understood that credit card debt was bad, but I didn't fully comprehend what my shoe habit would cost me until it was too late. I wish I had. It would have saved me a lot of stress and anxiety (and money!).

And that's the reality: If you send your kids out into the world without basic knowledge of things like how savings can grow, the importance of not spending more than you earn, et cetera, you're just setting them up for the kind of situation they'll have to spend years stressing to get out of, such as too much debt from student loans, zero savings for an emergency (and in that case, you can bet you're getting a phone call), or credit card bills galore. It's not fair to them to do that.

I'm not going to write a whole manifesto on how to teach your kids about money; there are tons of great books and online resources on the topic. But I will give you some rough rules I've picked up from parenting and personal finance experts over the years.

* **Give your kids an allowance.** Start at around five years old, basically as soon as they can count and understand the concept. As a very rough rule of thumb, give $1 per week for each year of your child's life (so a six-year-old would get $6 per week, a sixteen-year-old would get $16 per week), but don't get hung up on the amount. That matters less than the fact that you give it to them, and use it as a way to teach them about spending and saving. It's a good idea to make them

save at least some of their allowance. Give them an age-appropriate goal for where those savings will go, like some cool new paints for your three-year-old or a new Barbie for your ten-year-old. Littler kids should save in a clear container so they can watch the money grow. They should also go with you to buy that item, count out the money for it, and give it to the cashier themselves so they begin to learn how money works. And, it's also a good idea to allow kids to earn extra money by doing extra chores around the house; this shows them that doing more than the minimum can be rewarded.

* **Use everyday occurrences as teachable moments.** You don't necessarily need to sit down and have "money talks" very frequently, because money touches nearly every part of our lives—from when we go to the grocery store to heading off to work—and we can use those moments to pass on wisdom to the kids. If you're pulling out your credit card to pay for drinks at Starbucks, explain to the kids what a credit card is, and where the money comes from.

* **As kids get older, they need more sophisticated lessons.** Tweens should start really digging into the concept of delaying gratification. When they've saved a certain amount of money, they can get X now, or keep saving to get an even better item. It's a good idea to set teens up with a bank account, show them how compound interest works on a loan and teach them about credit cards. You don't want your child going off to college without this kind of knowledge; that's a financial train wreck waiting to happen—and one you'll likely have to clean up.

Lead by example. This is perhaps the most important of all. Kids watch how you and/or your spouse talk about and handle money. Be an example of someone who saves, who gives back to her community, who uses money as a way to produce joy in her life rather than as a way to accrue designer handbags. These are lessons kids will take with them into their own relationships and pass along to their own children.

Congratulations!

That's it! You've made it—have a drink (or two, I'm not judging!) to celebrate. You've now committed yourself to a financial plan that can and will help you spend less and save more—without driving yourself nuts! It's not going to be perfect every single week (life, it comes at ya!) and there will be setbacks, but if you just keep the course, you will be in a better place financially in a few months, in a few years, and when you retire. And that's worth a cheer or two!

Acknowledgments

There are so many people I'd like to thank, so here goes, in no particular order: My incredible husband and daughter; my editors Hannah Phillips and Christina Boys, who are both amazing at their jobs and a joy to work with; the entire team at Hachette; my agent Jill Marsal, whose spot-on insight helped shape the format for this book; my editors and colleagues at Dow Jones, including—but by no means limited to— Raakhee Mirchandani, Katerina Ang, Katie Vanneck-Smith, Jeremy Olshan, Quentin Fottrell, and Almar Latour; Soledad O'Brien, one of the most badass women in media and someone I've long looked up to in my career; fellow personal finance authors Kimberly Palmer, Emma Johnson, Liz Frugalwoods, Jean Chatzky, and Suze Orman, all of whom have written must-read books that I adored; Gracelyn Woods, whose friendship and support and love for my daughter have meant so much to me; Alexa Kaiser, who has been a dear friend and mentor for more than a decade now; Lauren Houdlett, who always knows how to make a bad day disappear (and loves margaritas as much as I do!); my mom friends, in particular Sarah Stonebly, who have shared their friendship and inspired many things in this book; all the family who have helped out as I was writing, including Maime and Papi, Grandma, Aunt Sushi, Grandpa, and Susan; Vivianne LaTouche; and Lindsey Stanberry. I also want to thank everyone at Dow Jones Media Group: It is through my years of reporting at Marketwatch, Moneyish, and SmartMoney that I learned so many of the money-saving tips in this book. Without that invaluable experience—and the editors who pushed me to dig deeper— this book would not have been possible.

About the Author

Catey Hill is a mom and journalist whose work has appeared in the *Wall Street Journal, SmartMoney, Worth, Seventeen,* the *New York Daily News,* MarketWatch.com, Forbes.com, and myriad other publications and websites. Catey has appeared as a personal finance and consumer expert on dozens of TV shows, including *Today, Fox & Friends, The Lead with Jake Tapper, The Huckabee Show,* and *CBS This Morning;* in a number of magazines and newspapers, including the *New York Times, Marie Claire, Allure, People, Seventeen, Cosmopolitan,* and *Woman's Day;* and on more than a hundred radio programs. She regularly appears on radio shows such as the nationally syndicated *This Morning: America's First News with Gordon Deal* and stations like KRLD Dallas and WDEL Delaware's News. Catey is also the author of *Shoo, Jimmy Choo! The Modern Girl's Guide to Spending Less and Saving More.* She lives in Brooklyn with her husband, daughter, and their cat, Mouse. You can read more about her and her work at CateyHill.com.